Potholes, Parks, and Politics
A Guide to Getting Things Done Locally
(Without Having to Run for Office Yourself)

by
Lisa R. Shaffer, Ph.D.
With help from Teresa Arballo Barth

Illustrations by Sharon Belknap

Potholes, Parks, and Politics

A Guide to Getting Things Done Locally
(Without Having to Run for Office Yourself)

by
Lisa R. Shaffer, Ph.D.

With help from Teresa Arballo Barth

Illustrations by Sharon Belknap

First Edition: October 2020
Printed in the United States of America
ISBN: 978-1-7358557-0-7

Library of Congress Control
Number: 2020923498

Table of Contents

PREFACE vii
SECTION 1
    CHAPTER 1: INTRODUCTION 1
    CHAPTER 2: DEFINE THE PROBLEM 6
    CHAPTER 3: IDENTIFY THE PLAYERS AND KNOW
                 THE RULES 12
    CHAPTER 4: WORKING WITH A CITY 16
    CHAPTER 5: PUTTING CONCEPTS INTO ACTION 21
    CHAPTER 6: BUILD THE CASE 30
    CHAPTER 7: GOING PUBLIC 36
    CHAPTER 7: WHAT NEXT? 42
    CLOSING THOUGHTS...47

SECTION 2
    DIGGING DEEPER 51

SECTION 3
    TOOLBOX...68
    IN CONCLUSION...87
    ABOUT THE AUTHORS...88
    ACKNOWLEDGEMENTS 92
    REFERENCES 92
    TERMINOLOGY 93

PREFACE

You want something fixed in your town. Maybe it's slowing down traffic in your neighborhood to protect kids at play. Maybe it's fixing the cracked, potholed street in front of your mother's house. The noise after midnight from that new bar on the next block is keeping you up at night. The nearest park to your daughter's house is miles out of her way so your grandchild doesn't get to use the swings as often as she should. Whatever it may be--faster police and ambulance response times, less development in the open lands of town, or something else—you are left with a question? What should you do?

Until these problems arose, you probably never thought about local government. You voted (maybe) for the city council candidates that your politically active neighbor recommended without spending a lot of time studying the candidates or the issues. But now you want something done. So, what to do?

This guidebook is an attempt by two former elected officials in a mid-sized city in Southern California to share what they learned from their experiences, adding background information and input from experts and others who have served at the local level, in a handbook we hope will be helpful to the everyday lives of people. This is not a guide to big city politics. It is not a critique of American democracy. It's a simple effort to answer the question "How do I get my local government to get something done in my community?"

The first part of the book uses three examples of everyday people who have a problem they think their city needs to address. The second section, Digging Deeper, goes into more detail about our governmental system, with particular attention to local government. It also addresses when and how to use the legal system. The last part is called the Toolbox and provides more in-depth information and sample documents for each step in the process of local civic problem-solving. The Appendix offers links to more resources for those interested in local government.

The authors bring different backgrounds and perspectives to this task, but they share the experience of winning election to the City Council of Encinitas, California, a city of about sixty thousand residents in the north coastal area of San Diego County. They reflected on who they listened to, who was effective in bringing new ideas and constructive proposals, and which residents went away frustrated and feeling like nobody cared. What made the difference?

Civility, clarity, and communication–those are the keys to success. People who had taken the time to clearly define the core issue, the real problem, that needed attention, did their homework, and were open to exploring a range of responses, were much more likely to be satisfied. Those who approached public officials in a spirit of collaboration and not confrontation were more likely to feel heard.

There is a lot of ignorance and misinformation in our society about local government, even though there is much truth in the adage that all politics is local. While broad policy is determined at the state and federal level, those policies become manifest in our towns and cities. Committing to reduce greenhouse gases is one thing. Whether a community chooses to meet that goal through encouraging more walking and bicycle travel; by mandating solar panels and graywater systems in new construction; by planting more trees; or any number of other strategies depends on local government actions or inactions.

This guidebook is meant to help people effectively advocate for whatever policies and programs they desire. It also provides some background and perspective to help people understand what is feasible, what is appropriate, and what to expect when they undertake such efforts.

SECTION 1

Chapter 1

INTRODUCTION

If you're lucky, most of the time, life is good. The streets are paved, clean water comes out of the tap, and traffic lights work. While we often think neighbors are too noisy, there's too much traffic, and taxes are too high, that's also what we think of as normal life.

Then something happens. Your trash doesn't get collected for two weeks straight; there's a big pothole that hasn't been filled; a serious accident highlights a dangerous intersection; or you hear that a multistory apartment building is going up in your single-family-home neighborhood. Suddenly you start paying attention and asking questions. Sometimes the situation moves you to get involved, to want to do something. This chapter provides a framework for determining what's really going on and what, realistically, you can do about it.

All politics may be local, but local government is not all-powerful. Quality of life consists of both the mundane aspects of living that are impacted, if not controlled at the local level--i.e., working, going to school, and enjoying recreation and culture. Overarching these are the big picture issues handled largely at the federal level, like the state of the economy, foreign relations, national security, and civil rights. Very few issues fall into neat, clear boxes labeled as city, county, state, or national responsibility. So, the first step in defining your problem and how to solve it is to understand what the real issue is and who has the authority to make changes.

Meet Jacinta, Matt, and Lee

Throughout this guidebook, we will discuss three scenarios. Each is drawn from real situations we encountered but they are not intended to represent any actual living persons or projects.

Jacinta saw landscape contractors spraying something in the median near her home, along a route where she walks with her two young children. She saw a different contractor spraying something in the local park. She is concerned about toxic chemicals and her children's health, as well as the potential impact on the environment. She wants public spaces to be maintained using natural products and not harmful pesticides.

Matt is unhappy because a vacant parcel of land near his home has been identified as a site for affordable housing. He heard it will be a multistory, multifamily complex. He's concerned about the impact on his property values as well as potential traffic impacts and increased crime.

Lee almost got hit by a speeding car when she was walking her dog over to a nearby park. She wants a stop sign on the corner of her street so she can feel safe crossing the street. She thinks the speed limit is too high and cars go too fast and it's too hard to get to the park.

Where to begin?

Jacinta has a clear understanding of what she wants. She started by calling the main number for her city government. Good move, Jacinta.

She asked for information—what was the city's policy on use of pesticides? Who were the city's landscape contractors? Where could she find copies of the contracts with those landscape companies? She also looked at the websites for her state environmental protection agency and for the federal EPA to see what pesticides were approved and which were banned for use in public spaces.

Jacinta knew that there are different levels of government. Each has its own set of responsibilities, but it is not always clear to ordinary residents who to call for what issue. In the case of environmental regulations, if something is banned at the federal level, it cannot be used anywhere, including her city. If something is not banned at the federal level, but is banned at the state level, her city should not be using it. If it is not banned at a higher level, it might still be prohibited in her city's policies. Jacinta was trying to answer her first question: *Is the problem that public officials are not following existing laws and regulations, or do laws or regulations have to be created or changed to get what she wants?*

Principle 1: Define the problem: Find out whether your issue is that existing laws aren't being followed; that existing laws need to be changed; or that there are no laws addressing the problem.

Matt decides to tackle the housing issue by sending an alarmist email to all his neighbors alerting them to what he perceives as an assault on community character. He encourages everyone to contact their city council representative and the mayor immediately to try to stop this monstrosity from being built, and he sends his own email expressing his outrage. The mayor and council members reply that the project meets state guidelines for special affordable housing privileges and is exempt from certain local zoning requirements. They also tell him that there were two public hearings about the project as well as a community forum where he could have learned more and expressed his views prior to approval. He learned that the developer did make some changes to accommodate input from the neighbors who attended and that further reviews are still to come.

Matt was not aware of how to get official information about local projects. He was not plugged in to the various notification services governments offer that alert residents to new project proposals and community forums. He was not on the mailing list for his state representatives who voted on new housing policies to encourage higher density, smaller designs to address the shortage of lower-priced options. Matt now has to figure out what he can still do about this project, given its current status.

Matt is typical of most residents. Until something grabs their attention, they have better things to do than monitor local government activities. It may be too late to influence some aspects of this project, but it's not too late to make a difference. By paying attention now, he'll also be in a better position the next time something is proposed that may impact him. With the right information, he can figure out when and how to intervene.

> Principle 2: Know the rules: Get enough information to understand the decision-making process so you can intervene at the right time for your issue.

Lee has a friend on the traffic commission. Your local government might have a citizen panel or group that reviews traffic and public safety concerns. Find out. Lee's town does, and she talked to her friend about her concerns. Her friend said the city council requires new traffic measures be reviewed first by the commission and suggested that Lee come to a commission meeting and make her case. She also suggested that Lee look at other traffic calming measures that the city has implemented to see if there are other ways to make it safe to get from Lee's corner to the park. It is important to know who, within your local government, has the power to make decisions or to offer recommendations. Then you can start getting educated and build your case with the right people.

Principle 3: Identify the players: Find out who has the authority to make recommendations and decisions about your issue, so you can advocate to the right people.

In these three scenarios, who do you think is most likely to prevail? First, let's see if we can clearly articulate what success looks like. Often, residents have a solution in mind that they are trying to achieve, but it's not always clear that their solution addresses the real underlying problem.

The following chapters in this section will guide you through getting the necessary information, determining who you need to talk to, how to build your case, and when and how to go public. Then you can Dig Deeper in Section 2 to learn more about how local government works. Section 3, the Toolbox, offers examples and more detailed guidance on taking the actions to see your issue resolved.

CHAPTER 2

DEFINE THE PROBLEM

Successful advocacy requires effort. There is homework involved. Think of it like a word problem in middle school math class. "Susie has seven oranges; Jamal is 6'2" tall. There are three days until Halloween. How fast was the bus going?" Just kidding. But like those actual word problems, the first step is to translate the story into a solvable equation--to lay out what you know and what you need to know to find the answer. Whether the solution is a new law, an appeal of a zoning decision, or a new crosswalk depends on how you define the problem.

This chapter focuses on local action, but the principles apply to advocacy at a school board, a regional organization, state, or federal government. The more you know, the better prepared you will be to achieve your goal. Let's see how our three residents are doing.

For Jacinta, the situation is pretty straightforward. Her ultimate goal is to be able to enjoy public spaces in her community without endangering her health or the health of her children. She has struggled with health issues and is very sensitive to environmental conditions. While the levels of toxic chemicals may be tolerable for some otherwise-healthy people, they are not for her. So she is extra vigilant and very motivated to make sure her community is safe for her, and other vulnerable people, to enjoy. The simplest way to achieve this goal is to ensure that dangerous chemicals are not used. Her challenge is not to define the goal, but to figure out how to make it happen.

Matt's concerns are more complex. Perhaps he has some underlying fear based on a false perception that low income housing will attract "undesirable" people. He has explicitly expressed concern about his property value and crime. He gives lip service to the housing problem--"I'm all for affordable housing. I know we need it. It's just that this location is not a good location for it."

Whether his focus on traffic is valid remains to be seen. Of course, more cars mean more traffic, but some roads are able to absorb more vehicles without significant impact and some aren't. Traffic impacts are also affected by the availability of public transit and safe sidewalks and bike lanes, especially for income-restricted housing where residents may not own cars at all or are not likely to own multiple cars as seen at larger homes.

Making Matt happy may not ever be possible. He may just not like the idea that a state agency can determine what can be built in his neighborhood. He may not even like the idea that the city cannot stop a project that meets municipal zoning requirements. He may be frustrated that he wasn't in the loop or feel like he had any voice in decisions he thinks will impact his quality of life.

For Matt to move forward constructively, he needs to dig deeper into his own motivations and figure out what he really needs to be satisfied, and whether that's a realistic goal. He may have to accept changes he doesn't like and find ways to have some influence. For example, if he accepts that the project is going forward, there may be opportunities to provide input on the final design, the landscaping, and the location of driveways and sidewalks. Perhaps he can try to push for some offsets from the developer that could enhance Matt's neighborhood like a new pocket park or a bike lane or a bus stop. At the very least, maybe he can save some big beautiful trees.

Stop signs are one way to manage traffic flow. However, Lee, not being trained in circulation management (a fancy way of saying figuring out where traffic should go), may be frustrated if she focuses only on a stop sign. To the average person, it seems an obvious solution. But in reality, there are surprisingly complex rules for when and where stop signs can be placed-- rules that can come from the local, state and even the federal level.

If instead she realizes that her actual goal is to have a way to safely get to the park, the city might be better able to take action. For example, in cases where there is only intermittent need to cross the street, a stop sign may be inefficient, adding to auto emissions from stopping and starting, and allowing drivers to become lax and slide through the intersection when they don't see any pedestrians. A pedestrian-activated crosswalk with flashing lights might make more sense, so cars can continue when there's no need to stop.

Perhaps narrowing the width of the street and introducing curves and other elements to slow traffic would be sufficient to allow safe crossing. But that is a capital improvement project that requires significant funding. Or maybe Lee needs to push to have better connectivity of sidewalks that would allow her to go to the nearest signalized intersection that already is in place. It might feel like a clear and visible victory to see a bright shiny red octagon on her corner, and like a failure if she has to walk a few blocks extra to get to a safe crossing. From the perspective of the community, however, the balance of interests between greenhouse gas emissions (yes, everything is ultimately a climate issue), vehicular traffic efficiency, and both car and pedestrian safety, as well as other budget priorities, the best solution might look different. If Lee can recognize this, she will be more effective in her efforts. Lee wants to get herself and her dog safely to the park, but she needs to be flexible about how to accomplish that.

For big, complex issues, particularly involving land use, zoning, and development, it may be wise to consult an attorney specializing in local issues at the start of your efforts. We hope that by following our advice you will prevail without resorting to the courts. However, even without any lawsuits being filed, there are complicated laws governing decision-making processes and public participation. If you have good guidance at the start, you may avoid common mistakes, such as missing a deadline for an appeal or submitting your comments to the wrong office or in the wrong format. It may cost a few thousand dollars to have an attorney on retainer, or you may be able to find someone with appropriate legal knowledge who will give you preliminary advice *pro bono.* What you should know from the start is that if you end up in litigation, it is stressful, expensive, unpredictable, and not fun. Finding a resolution without the courts is always preferred. In Section 2, you can **Dig Deeper** 🔍 to find information on when and how to use a lawyer.

Winning Isn't Everything

Sometimes challenging the status quo can spotlight
a deficiency in policy and practice that can't be corrected
immediately, but your efforts can lay the groundwork for
larger political efforts to come.

Where to Find Information

 Policies and practices don't appear out of nowhere. There's a reason, explicit or unstated, why conditions are what they are - why your problem exists. In order to make change, start with trying to understand the status quo. It may be that there already exists a law or policy that would accomplish what you want, but it is not being implemented. It may be that what you want is prohibited by laws or policies that would have to be modified or repealed to achieve your goal. And it may be that your situation evolved outside of any regulatory framework and either intentionally or through neglect, has been allowed to continue without rules or regulations. It is important for you to understand which of these conditions applies to your situation.

Your local library and the reference librarian can often help you with basic information and access to databases and online resources. Within your local jurisdiction, the city government is the best place to understand what laws and regulations already exist, related to your issue. Don't be afraid to ask what you think may be "dumb questions." The only dumb questions are the ones you wish you had asked but were afraid to. Your tax dollars pay the salaries of the people working in your city hall, and generally speaking, they know that they work for you. If you are reasonable and respectful, you can get a lot of help at city hall.

The **Toolbox** ✕ describes how to get information from online resources as well as the people who work for you in city hall.

Government doesn't move fast by design, there are often multiple and sometimes competing agencies that have to weigh-in on the project. If there is a solution that has already been implemented in your city or nearby, you will have a much easier time.

CHAPTER 3

IDENTIFY THE PLAYERS AND KNOW THE RULES

Unless you know how the system works and who has the authority to do what you are seeking, you might direct your efforts in the wrong direction. Your issue may be completely within the jurisdiction and control of your local government. Or not. Laws are made at federal, state, and local level. Sometimes this is clear; at other times courts are needed to determine which level of government has what power. Often there are overlapping rules and regulations.

You can **Dig Deeper** ⚲ into the "Levels of Government" in Section 2, which provides more details. What is important is to know who has the power to do what you are asking.

> "The powers not delegated to the United States by the Constitution, nor prohibited by it to the states, are reserved to the states respectively, or to the people."
>
> --United States Constitution, 10th Amendment

In general, cities have authority as defined in their state's constitution. Some jurisdictions are charter cities (as opposed to general law cities) and develop their own charter defining their structure and duties. States have different procedures for authorizing charter cities and modifications to their charters. Either way, there is always some degree of state control that a city is subject to, and some degree of autonomy. When dealing with complex issues such as housing, issues of power and jurisdiction can often end up in the courts.

For most cities, local attention tends to focus on public safety (fire, police), traffic, and land use (who gets to build what where). But environmental concerns from trash collection and recycling to climate action plans are increasing in visibility and importance as well.

This guidebook focuses on how to get things done at the local level, and for that, we need to look at the local government and its elected body, generally called the city council or county board, that sets policy; approves budgets; and hires the city/county manager or chief administrator, the day-to-day operational leader of the municipality. Cities can have either a strong mayor who has independent authority to take action and works with administrative staff directly, or a weak mayor system in which the mayor and council hire a city manager and the manager oversees operations consistent with budgets and policy guidance approved by the elected council or board.

The key to your success as an advocate is to know where the authority lies to take the action you are seeking - who's at the table and how does the game work. It might seem overwhelming, but you can figure it out.

Stakeholders

Once you determine that you are at the right level of government and know the bare bones of your issue --whether or not there is existing law or policy--you can start to think about who the stakeholders are in your particular case. A stakeholder is a person or organization that has an interest, or stake, in the issue. It is an entity that will be impacted, positively or negatively, by the change you are seeking. And as a result, understanding who your stakeholders are can help you find allies and possibly convert adversaries.

Ask why things are the way they are. Do specific individuals or groups have an interest in keeping it that way? Did someone already work hard to have a rule enacted? Is this a "hot topic" or something arcane or limited that only a few folks would care about? Are there individuals or groups working on your issue right now?

The basic question you need to ask is who stands to gain and who will lose if your recommendations are enacted. Typically, there are winners and losers whenever there is change. Understanding the stakes can help you plan an effective advocacy strategy.

Maybe it's a minimal impact, like the embarrassment of being called out for not following existing policy. Consider plastic, candy-filled Easter eggs. In our city, every spring there was an egg hunt in a city park and kids searched for cheap, made-in-China disposable eggs. Someone asked why we were spending public money to buy plastic junk that would end up in the landfill when, already on the books, was an environmentally preferred purchasing policy.

Our city had enacted the policy years earlier, and with changing staff and leadership, it had been forgotten or overlooked. Once the policy was brought to light, departments could now justify choosing the giveaways for the spring egg hunt from the recycled products catalog rather than the cheap (and cheaper) plastic made-in-China throwaways that would just end up in the landfill. They were happy to make this change but hadn't realized they could use criteria other than cost to choose the eggs. No public hearings, no votes required.

In areas where there is a citizen commission, like traffic or parks, be sure to check in with them to see what their views are. You can find commission members, contact information, and minutes from past meetings online in most cities. If you have trouble, check with the city manager or city clerk. Staff and commissioners are all stakeholders.

CHAPTER 4

WORKING WITH A CITY

They say all politics is local, but what does local mean? Lisa offers this illustration.

I live in an incorporated city, which means that the state granted residents the right to form their own local government. Prior to incorporation, decisions were made by the county government, which covers a far greater area with much less direct local representation. Thus, the developer who built my house had to have a building permit from the city. (Since my city is relatively new, incorporated in 1986, structures built before incorporation had to get permits from the county, which had different rules.)

The developer who built my house also needed a Coastal Development Permit from the California Coastal Commission, a state agency, since my area is within the official definition of the Coastal Zone and there is a state law giving the Coastal Commission authority to review and approve development along the ocean. Children in my neighborhood go to an elementary school managed by one school district, and then move to middle and high school under the jurisdiction of a different school board. Both school districts include portions of other cities and my city has schools not in either school district.

My drinking water is provided by a water district that is a separate legal entity from the city but whose board of directors is the same as the local city council. However, people in another part of the city get their water from a different water authority. If that's not confusing enough, my city provides some of its public services directly--we manage our own fire department--but it also serves two adjacent, smaller cities that couldn't afford the investment needed to have their own agency. My city, however, contracts with the county for police services from the county sheriff's department because it was deemed impractical to operate our own police department. The interstate highway that bisects the town is the responsibility of a federal and state transportation agency. And the list could go on and on.

DID YOU KNOW?

In an analysis of the 25 largest metropolitan areas in the US, as of 2002, San Diego was the least politically fragmented of them all, with one county, 18 cities, and 0.7 local governments per 100,000 residents. At the other end of the spectrum, the Chicago metro area has 13 counties and 567 local governments, with 6.6 governments per 100,000 residents. Pittsburgh has 17.7 local governments per 100,000, with 418 different local governments in six counties.[1]

Yes, it's complicated. Each local government has a unique history and a complex network of relationships with other jurisdictions and special districts. This is why our basic principles apply - you have to figure out how the system works and who the players are before you go farther.

When I was running for a seat on the city council, I shouldn't have been surprised if people were unclear about exactly what the Encinitas City Council is and what it does. My city is relatively young, and some people weren't even sure if they lived in the city or not. Like it or not, most people don't pay any attention until a problem arises and they want to see something happen. THEN they need to know.

Shortly after I moved into my house, a delivery truck accidentally backed into a fire hydrant across the street and sent a gushing stream of water into the air. I called 911. The operator asked what water district I was in. I had no idea. At the time, I didn't even know there was more than one. If I had been able to give the right answer quickly, I would have saved many gallons and a lot of landscaping! But until that time when you need to know, you don't need to know. Unfortunately, in this case, the need arose rather quickly!

Everything I Needed to Know about Local Government I Learned in 3rd Grade.

In general, if you live in an incorporated city, you have a city council. Some are "at large," meaning that all the representatives are elected by voters throughout the city, and some bigger cities have geographic districts with one representative from each district. Cities either have a strong mayor, who serves as the chief executive and oversees staff, or they have a weak mayor/city manager form of government, where the day-to-day operations are managed by a career employee who is accountable to the city council. In both configurations, the idea is to have the elected officials set policy and approve a budget, presumably reflecting the priorities and values of the voters who elected them, while the actual work of paving roads and maintaining sewers and managing traffic is done by professional staff. When you have an issue, or you're looking for information, it's important to know who's in charge of the thing you care about.

Every year in California, third graders study local government as part of the state curriculum. (Sadly, most have forgotten it all by high school, and certainly by adulthood!) Some schools bring their classes to city hall for a mock council meeting. The students develop proposals and take positions for and against. The year that we opened a new public park, students came to debate whether there should have been a swimming pool in the park. Some said that since we are a coastal city with lovely beaches, there was no need for a pool. Others thought we needed the pool for swimming lessons so kids would be safe going to the beach.

Then we talked about how to pay for the pool. One group of students advocated for a swim-up, all-you-can-eat ribs bar to provide the revenues to pay for the pool. It's unlikely our city will see that food service any time soon, but decisions about parks and recreation programs are a city council responsibility. The council allocates

funds and sets priorities across different sectors—replacing a sewer main, building a new lifeguard tower, paving more streets, or including a swimming pool in a new community park.

Some students proposed an educational program in the schools about the evils of junk food. They learned that they were talking to the wrong audience. Curriculum is the domain of the school district, governed by its elected school board. Public health is handled at the county level. On the other hand, the city could help by being a good role model and removing junk food from vending machines at city buildings and parks and public events sponsored by the city.

Every Level Matters

It never hurts to make your issue known, and to provide educational information at all levels of decision-making. If someone brings an issue to the city council that isn't within their purview, but captures their interest and support, the council can weigh in with other bodies. Letters go from the mayor to county, state or federal representatives expressing support or opposition to legislation being considered at their level, and it doesn't hurt to get their help on your issue, too, wherever the authority lies. But allocate your time and energy appropriately, with the most energy where the most authority lies. You can **Dig Deeper** ⚲ into levels of government in Section 2.

Do partisan politics affect city governments? The answer is "yes." Filling potholes are not a particularly Republican or Democratic issue—members of both parties want them filled in. But *how* you fill them in, *who* should fill them in and *who* should pay for it? Republicans and Democrats may answer those questions very differently. Beliefs about the role of government, what should be publicly funded and what should be left to the private and non-profit sectors, and related values do matter in how local government decisions are made and budgets are allocated.

Whether or not your city council is technically nonpartisan, some, if not all, of the elected officials will be officially or unofficially affiliated with one party or the other. It's good to be aware of that. However, it is also true that people of all political persuasions drive on city streets and breathe the air and take their kids to the local parks and playgrounds. The more you can remove any political overlay from your own advocacy and work to make those who support you into heroes in the community, the more likely you are to find success.

CHAPTER 5

PUTTING CONCEPTS INTO ACTION

Jacinta, Matt, and Lee

To get back to our examples, Jacinta wants to keep cancer-causing chemicals out of public spaces. She does her homework and finds that, indeed, the city's municipal code section and related regulation say pesticides should only be used if they are on a specific list developed by city staff and only as a last resort for as short a time as possible. When pesticides are used, the contractor must post warning flags with information about what was sprayed and when, and must report usage to the city regularly. Jacinta has hit the jackpot. She asks for copies of reports from landscape contractors and finds there aren't any recent ones, even though she saw the warning flags and actually stopped and asked the contractors what product they were using. It was one on the list that has to be reported.

Now Jacinta has two issues. First, existing policies are not being followed and it doesn't seem that staff is paying enough attention to notice. She wants existing policies to be enforced--i.e., a change in practice. Second, she doesn't think there is a need for these chemicals at all, whether properly posted or not. She wants to change the current policy.

The first part can be handled without a big public fuss, she hopes. She doesn't want to shame anyone--she just wants to protect people's health. She hopes that by pointing out the problem to the relevant staff and copying their boss, she can get them to start paying attention and bring awareness to the contractors of their reporting obligation.

To make a change in the policies, she needs to ask who the stakeholders are for this issue. The companies that make the pesticides want to push sales, for sure. The landscape contractors want to keep their city contracts. The city staff who administer those contracts and are responsible for parks and medians want to satisfy their boss, the city manager, who wants to satisfy the city council and the public. The parks and recreation commission is supposed to represent the residents in advising the city council and staff, so it's good to check in with them, too. They are probably unaware of this issue and will want to play a role. It's a fairly safe bet that most residents would agree that they don't want to be exposed to carcinogens.

So why are these chemicals used in the first place? To prevent or kill weeds and keep parks and medians looking green and well landscaped. As with virtually all public policy issues, there are

tradeoffs. Implicitly or explicitly, we use cost-benefit analysis to help inform our decisions--what is the risk of causing cancer compared to the benefit of attractive public spaces?

What Jacinta needs to do is reframe the issue--can we have attractive public spaces without cancer-causing chemicals? Can she propose a win-win for everyone or almost everyone? Can she limit any reasons anyone would have to oppose her proposed change? Fortunately, through her involvement with environmental education and advocacy groups, she knows there are organic options available and sets her sights on transitioning the city to an all-organic parks management policy.

For Matt's issue, it's not so simple. Affordable housing is a very complex issue with many stakeholders and a lot of politics, money, emotions, and regulation. Matt needs to sort out what authority the city has, and whether to try to intervene at the state level on housing policy, or work at the margins locally.

Matt has retreated into study mode. He was embarrassed at his initial attempt to arouse support and block the development. He signs up for notices from his city-- most cities have online distribution lists that allow you to get email when there is an upcoming event, whether it is a city  council meeting, or a planning commission hearing, and so on. The image below is from the borough of Manasquan, New Jersey, and shows the options to sign up for alerts from their borough.

Residents can enroll in any or all of the following categories:

☑ **Emergency Alerts**
This includes high priority emergency notifications from the Office of Emergency Management (evacuation orders, critical notifications, emergency information). Subscribers are strongly urged to activate email, text and phone alerts for this subscription in order to ensure that critical emergency messages are not missed.

☑ **Borough News, Bulletins & Events**
This includes all general information from the Borough including news and upcoming events, meeting information, fundraisers as well as information from various municipal departments and groups, including construction/code, finance, environmental, tourism, shade tree, etc.

☑ **Weather Alerts**
This includes hazardous weather advisories issued for Manasquan by the National Weather Service.

☑ **Coastal Flood Warnings**
This includes alerts from Stevens Flood Advisory system (provides up to 4 day notice of expected flood conditions in Manasquan) as well as coastal flood alerts from the National Weather Service.

☑ **Traffic Advisories**
This includes notices of road & bridge closures, construction detours, and special events.

☑ **Law Enforcement Alerts**
This includes alerts from the Manasquan Police Department.

☑ **Beach Information**
This includes beach and ocean conditions, activities and events.

☑ **Public Works / Recycling**
This includes information on recycling, garbage, leaf pick-up, fire hydrant flushing, etc. from our Public Works Department.

He also found an online tracking system on his city's website that gives the status of all proposed projects going through the permitting process. He can search by location or type of project, so he can find other potentially problematic projects. He decides to focus first on his own education and starts attending meetings of the planning commission.

A planning commission meeting is usually the first public airing of new building proposals. Developers submit project plans to city staff to start the process. The staff works with applicants to try to ensure that projects meet city codes, and then, depending on the complexity and size of the project, staff can either approve them directly, or require a public hearing before the planning commission. Public notices are published in local newspapers and on the city website to inform residents of hearings; signs are posted on the site of the proposed project (this is how Matt initially learned about his project); and the agenda for the planning commission includes details of the proposed project and the staff's recommendations for approval, denial, or modification.

Matt learns that some of the information he found on a neighborhood blog was wrong. He finds that while the overall scope of the project in his neighborhood meets current state and local requirements, an environmental analysis, design review, and a traffic mitigation plan are all needed before the final approval is given.

[NOTE: this is not the case for all affordable housing projects-- some states allow developers to bypass some or all of these steps in the interest (theoretically at least) of reducing cost and expediting construction of needed low-income housing].

Matt now has several opportunities to weigh in and potentially impact the final look of the project and how its traffic will be directed onto local streets. Usually big projects are required to make road modifications or pay into a traffic impact fund to offset the increased traffic projected from their development.

Matt learns that traffic will enter and exit away from his immediate vicinity, and that the traffic analysis says there will be no significant impacts on his preferred routes. He realizes he would have to hire competing traffic analysts to challenge that analysis. He decides instead that he will focus on the appearance of the new project, to try to make sure it looks like the surrounding homes and will try to ensure that mature trees currently on the vacant parcel are preserved.

Just like Jacinta had to do, Matt needs to think about stakeholders. Who is likely to be pushing for this project; who might share some of Matt's concerns? In addition to meeting with city staff, if he can, Matt should try to meet with the developer. Matt could explain that he missed the previous meetings and hope the developer would share the materials that were presented there, and answer some of Matt's questions. He could try to talk to all the planning commissioners, not just the one who represents his area, if they are chosen by districts. Approvals require a majority vote on the commission, so Matt will need to convince more than one commissioner once he knows what he wants to propose.

Major housing projects often attract lobbyists and advocates from the construction industry, as well as environmental activists, sometimes in partnership and sometimes in opposing roles. Matt would be well served to find out who has already taken a position by looking at who spoke at the public hearings, monitoring social media, and looking at any websites related to the project or to local housing issues.

Matt can also look for advocates related to design and to the environment. Groups like the Sierra Club or local garden clubs might want to help preserve the trees. If there are homeowners' associations in the area, he might connect with them, hoping they will see value in having appropriate design standards for new construction in their vicinity. By looking at the issue from many perspectives, he may be able to find ways to meet his objectives by framing this as a community service--to protect trees and the "look and feel" of the area on behalf of all the residents.

Lee's prospects depend, in part, on the culture in her city's transportation staff. Focusing traffic staff on pedestrian infrastructure and safety (and not just vehicles) may be a change from the way older staff were trained. Current employees, maybe some who have been there for a while and are quite comfortable in their positions, may have to retool to be able to design roadways that accommodate bicycles and pedestrians with equal attention to cars. When the traffic engineer got his training, the focus was on efficient movement of vehicles. He is going to have to take some classes or bring in other experts in order to implement new "complete streets" policies. For some, this is an exciting opportunity. For others, it just means more work.

While the benefits of complete streets may seem obvious to residents, especially those who walk and ride bikes, changing policy disrupts the existing order within the department where the change actually has to take place. Finding incentives for the staff so they feel that enthusiasm will be important. While this is the job of the city manager, if residents recognize the challenge and allow time to build support, you might have a better outcome long-term.

Lee finds the link on the city's website to past agendas and minutes from the traffic commission. She asks her friend on the commission to suggest examples of traffic calming that have already been approved (it's always easier to be the second project approved than the first). She also decides to research whether there have been previous accidents at her corner and discovers that information is not easy to find.

Lee sends a message to her neighbors asking if they have seen or been involved in accidents in their neighborhood, especially on the corner, and asking whether they would support a request for a stop sign.

She also searches the internet for "stop sign requirements." Her search takes her to the ***Manual on Uniform Traffic Control Devices for Streets and Highways***, or **MUTCD**, which "defines the standards used by road managers nationwide to install and maintain traffic control devices on all public streets, highways, bikeways, and private roads open to public travel. The MUTCD is published by the Federal Highway Administration (FHWA) under 23 Code of Federal Regulations (CFR), Part 655, Subpart F."[3] (We told you nothing is simple!) This scintillating document is the reason we have consistent size, shape, and color for road signs, among other things. It is also the code that local transportation planners must follow.

Stop signs aren't so simple, Lee learns. The MUTCD says, among other things:

> STOP signs should not be used for speed control.

> STOP signs should be installed in a manner that minimizes the numbers of vehicles having to stop. At intersections where a full stop is not necessary at all times, consideration should be given to using less restrictive measures such as YIELD signs . . .

Once the decision has been made to install two-way stop control, the decision regarding the appropriate street to stop should be based on engineering judgment. In most cases, the street carrying the lowest volume of traffic should be stopped.

Based on this information, Lee takes a walk around her neighborhood and surrounding communities to see if there are some other possibilities. She realizes that her real goal is to get safely to the park. If she prevailed with a stop sign, it would be her street that would be stopped, not the busier street she wants to cross. With a new perspective and lots of possibilities, she is ready to approach the city.

She decides to start where the action is, with the city traffic engineer. She finds his name and contact information on the city website and requests an appointment. To her surprise, he answers quickly and says he's happy to meet. City staff usually welcome appropriate interactions with members of the public. They chose their careers, generally speaking, because they want to solve problems and serve the public. If they have a chance to educate people and work with them to make things better, that's satisfying.

At their meeting, Lee is able to ask lots of questions and show the engineer pictures of different traffic calming measures she's seen. She wants to understand how he sees things, and to learn some of the vocabulary and key concepts. He is surprisingly nice and wants to help her find a solution.

How to Talk to Staff

Note that not all city staff are such warm, helpful people. As in any organization, there are people who may be having a bad day, who may be unhappy with their jobs, who may feel outdated because their area of expertise has evolved well past their own competence, or for any other reason could be difficult for a member of the public to work with.

If your Google education on the issue has identified possible solutions that the staff person doesn't mention, it's ok to ask something like "I saw that in another city they tried XYZ and it seems to be working. Are you familiar with that?" It could be that the staff person already knew about it and can explain to you why that example doesn't apply to your case. But it may be news to the staff, and something they could investigate.

If you find that the first staff person you encountered was not helpful or was unresponsive, you have the option of escalating to his or her boss. Your goal should not be to attack the staff, but to focus on what you are trying to accomplish. You can say something as vague as, "I tried working with the traffic engineer, but I wasn't able to find what I needed. Is there someone else I could talk to?" It might help. Or you might just have hit a poorly run department that isn't customer oriented. It happens.

What is important is that, before you escalate to a higher level, you make a good faith effort to do your homework, find the facts, think hard about what your real motivation and goals are, and stay focused on your task. You should also consider making an appointment with the city manager once you have done your homework and ask them the same questions you asked the staff. Sometimes you really do have to push and be persistent to get the bureaucracy to change its approach. It's always good to give them the opportunity to make the change you seek and think it was their idea, if possible. And remember: civility, clarity, and communication. These are the keys to your success.

CHAPTER 6

BUILD THE CASE

Congratulations. You have applied the principles in Chapter One: you defined the problem; you figured out the rules; and you identified the players. Now it's time to build your case, form alliances, and reach out if needed.

 In the best-case scenario, you have discovered that what you wanted to happen is what should have been happening all along--the laws and policies already require what you want, and the city just wasn't paying attention. Until you showed up. Maybe it turns out that because there is a school or a senior facility in your neighborhood, the speed limit should have been reduced to twenty-five miles per hour during school hours, something you had wanted to see on your street that is posted at thirty-five miles per hour and normally finds cars going forty-five or faster. Maybe the city staff has the authority already to post the twenty-five-mile-per-hour limit and to ask local law enforcement to issue warnings to help drivers learn about the change and pay attention to their speed.

Maybe, as in Jacinta's case, there is a policy requiring reports on pesticide use, which is a first step in her pursuit of pesticide-free parks, and now the staff has been reminded to insist on getting those reports from its landscape contractors.

For issues that seem likely to be approved based on your discussions with staff, your job may be done. Give the staff a chance to make the changes you discussed. Ask them for a timeline--when should you expect to see changes in landscape contracts; when should you expect reports on pesticide usage; and so on. Then follow up.

Assuming your efforts to date have not resolved the issue or led to the changes you desire, it's time for advocacy. You have educated yourself as much as you could. Now it's time to build alliances and engage with decision-makers and make your case. Once you are sure you understand, as much as possible, why things are the way they are, who the stakeholders are, and what changes might bring resolution to your concerns, you are ready to take action.

A vital aspect of advocacy is understanding where opposition might come from. How can you convert as many stakeholders as possible into allies? How can you engage people who would support you if they were aware but haven't been involved? Ideally you want to find a win-win solution, and that may require you to be flexible and realistic in setting your expectations. This is part of your advocacy strategy.

Case Statement

Put together your case statement--what is the issue, why does it matter, how can solving your problem make the community a better place. It isn't just about you--whatever action a city takes can create a precedent, so think beyond your own special circumstances (and we know, you ARE special, but still . . .) Try to imagine what the person you're talking to might think about it. Do you have the public interest in mind? Will supporting you make the public official a hero or a villain? How can you make this a winning issue for them?

What resources are needed to implement your solution? If additional personnel or money are required, are you proposing to reallocate resources, are you asking for additional resources, or are you proposing a solution that will pay for itself through fees or savings? Like the all-you-can-eat swim-up bar at the pool. A genius idea!!! Recognize that some solutions are easier than others, depending on whether it just takes a new focus, a shift in attention, or a significant investment of new resources. The **Toolbox** ✎ has a *sample Case Statement* that can help you think through all the issues.

Jacinta, Matt, and Lee

For Jacinta, the case is pretty clear. If pesticides are eliminated from public spaces, everyone will be safer, and everyone's  risk of cancer is reduced. For Matt, it's a more complicated case. People who are seeking affordable housing will benefit from the project. Employers who have trouble attracting low-wage workers because of the high cost of housing stand to gain. Construction means jobs. New housing means new property taxes which support the city budget. So affordable housing has many proponents. However, if Matt has refined his issue to design and landscape, especially saving big trees, his issues will have much less potential opposition, and he can possibly attract a broad set of supporters. His original goal of stopping the project altogether just may not be realistic.

Lee figures nobody is going to advocate for unsafe streets or dangerous intersections. However, she realizes that commuters like unimpeded routes and environmentalists understand that frequent stops and acceleration make cars inefficient and increase greenhouse gas emissions. (Environmentalists, though, also support alternatives to driving, so safe walking routes and crossings could appeal to them.) Traffic experts say that at intersections where most of the time there is no cross-traffic or pedestrians stop signs are likely to make conditions less safe, as drivers stop paying attention.

At this point, you are in the strategic planning stage. Make a list of who might support your ideas and who might oppose them. See if there are ways to modify your proposal or add to it to offset potential opposition. In other words, think about flexibility and incrementalism, so you have some alternatives or some options as you move forward.

For example, is there a way to start small with a pilot project to demonstrate the value of your proposal? If you wanted to ban the distribution of single-use plastic bags, you could have a phased implementation, giving businesses time to use existing inventory, and give away free cloth bags to help people make the transition.

Jacinta wants to stop all pesticide use. But she would be happy with starting by making one park pesticide-free and letting people see that it can still be beautifully maintained, without increasing costs. Matt doesn't really have a phased strategy option, since he's focused on one housing project. But he needs to see his efforts as setting a precedent, possibly, for future projects, and should expect interest and engagement from developers and residents in other areas that are anticipating similar projects and similar concerns. Lee might find willingness to try certain traffic calming measures on a temporary basis, like plastic speed humps that can be removed or a flashing sign that shows the speed of passing cars and reminds them of the speed limit.

Write down your case statement. Seriously. Treat it like a term paper. If you can't write it down clearly, you're not ready to present it to decision-makers. In the **Toolbox** ✎ there is a simplified example of a written case statement.

Once you have your case statement, you know what you want and why it matters. You have thought about who else cares, including those who might resist change. You've tried to consider multiple viewpoints and how your problem could be solved in a way that reduces or eliminates the negative impacts on possible opponents. You've talked to the relevant staff and gotten as much progress as they are able and willing to deliver. If it's still not enough, it's time for your political education to begin.

Meeting One-on-One with Public Officials

It's usually fairly straightforward to request an appointment with an elected official or a commission member. Most city websites have contact information, either a general number or direct links to each elected official. Commissions generally have a staff person who serves as liaison to the public members and can help you arrange meetings.

The **Toolbox** ✎ gives guidance on how to use your case statement to present your issue to the decision-makers when you meet privately with each one.

Every vote counts

Ask to meet with every decision-maker--don't assume you know their positions. Individual meetings with decision-makers gives them a chance to ask questions and consider your ideas.

Elected officials deserve a chance to learn about and consider your issue before being publicly called upon to take action. While some may choose not to make time for such a meeting, they should appreciate having been asked. Similarly, city staff can be better prepared to respond to questions from elected officials if staff have had a chance to hear your issue and answer your questions ahead of time. Nobody likes being blind-sided, especially politicians!

Make sure you stay focused on the issue, not your ego. It might be that a commissioner or an elected official takes your idea and pushes it without giving you the credit you think you deserve. That's OK. The point is to get the change you're advocating, and you will get further if you are not seeking the spotlight. If pushing for your issue makes some public official and/or staff look good, that's success.

If, however, after your meetings, you still haven't resolved your issue, the next step is to go public.

CHAPTER 7

GOING PUBLIC

Some issues cannot be resolved at the staff level. If you are asking for a change in policy or proposing a new approach, you will need the approval of elected officials through an open, public process. This starts by getting on the agenda.

Typically, decision-making bodies operate according to open government rules that vary state-to-state and locality-to-locality but with some general principles. The public is entitled to know when a deliberative body is going to take up a particular topic. This means the agenda is published in advance of a meeting so the public can be notified. This is where it matters that you have signed up for such notices through your city or county website. You can speak on anything at any meeting, but the council won't be able to take action until you get your issue on their published agenda.

Before you decide to speak at a public meeting, watch a session or two to get a sense of how it works. You can either watch archived video of past meetings or go in person and just sit in the audience. The more comfortable you are with the setting and process, the easier it will be for you to be an effective advocate.

Members of the public are entitled to speak at a public meeting. There are two types of public comments allowed--those specific to an agenda item, and non-agenda comments.

Before You Get on the Agenda

If you want to speak about something not on the agenda, there is generally a period of time for such comments, with time limits on each speaker and sometimes limits on overall time for those inputs. Typically, non-agenda comments are heard first, but no action can be taken other than to consider whether an item needs to come back as an agenda item at a future meeting after the required public notice. Remember, everyone has the right to know when an issue is being considered so they can take part. If a member of the public is asking for information, not action, the chief administrator or mayor may ask staff to follow up directly. It's frustrating when you want action now, but this is how our system works, to ensure that everyone who has an interest also has a chance to participate.

If you have been unable to get your issue on an agenda, speaking during the general public comment period can be a way of raising visibility. Maybe all that is needed is a nudge - a brief summary of the issue and a polite request for the council to put this on a future agenda. Sometimes a public official wants to do something but doesn't want to be seen as initiating the conversation, so having a resident ask for action provides the "cover" for the elected official to request an agenda item.

If your request is not addressed, if your item is not put on an agenda, you may want to go back to any potentially supportive staff person or council member and ask what you can do to get it there. While the city manager and mayor typically make the final decisions about the agenda, a staff person can push for something to be on an agenda, too. If you can uncover the source of resistance, you can try to address it. Maybe it is on a list of future action items but there is a long list ahead of you. In that case, you need to balance patience with persistence. See if you can get a commitment of when your item will be heard. If there is some urgency to your issue, be prepared to make the case for why it can't wait.

After pushing behind the scenes, if you still haven't gotten on the agenda, it doesn't hurt to try again during public comment. Remind the council that you requested this X weeks ago and have not yet seen it on an agenda. Explain why it matters. Show that you have many other residents (i.e., voters) also eager to see the issue addressed. Perhaps choose someone else to make the second request, referring to your initial effort.

> "Honorable mayor and council members, three weeks ago, my colleague, Terrence, requested that you put the issue of [turf for the soccer field; safe paths to the park; use of harmful chemicals in our public spaces . . .] on the agenda. So far, it has not happened. When I checked with the city clerk and city manager, they indicated that no specific date has been set. We recognize that you have many demands on your time. But, the 250 residents who signed the petition supporting XYZ [or the parents of the 125 soccer team members, etc.] are eager to see our city prioritize [public health, reducing soccer injuries, avoiding pedestrian accidents, . . .] so we respectfully request that you expedite consideration of this issue. Thank you.

Speaking to an Agenda Item

Once you get on the agenda and have a chance to make your case to the city council or the planning commission in a public meeting, be respectful. Throughout this whole process, it pays to remember we are all people with imperfections and feelings. Civility matters. Treating allies and opponents with care and respect is important--we all live in the same community and have more to our relationships than just this issue you are working on. Nothing turns off a prospective supporter more than a resident criticizing or shaming them in public. Members of the public are sometimes emotional and angry, and come to the microphone filled with hostility.

Imagine you are sitting on the dais and you hear something like this:

"You council members are all corrupt. You are in the pockets of the developers, just chasing your next campaign contribution. You don't care about the people of our city. If you did, you'd [stop this project; ban pesticides; put in a stop sign; approve artificial turf for the soccer field . . .].

If you were on the dais, and had not yet decided about this issue, would this kind of behavior make you want to vote yes? If you were a resident thinking of joining forces on this issue, would you want to work with that speaker? Instead, consider the impact of a public speaker who approached the microphone like this:

"Honorable council members, my name is Ethan Jones and I have lived in MyTown for fifteen years. Thank you for your service. You have one of the toughest jobs around! I appreciate your time and the time each of you took to meet with me prior to tonight's meeting. I am here to ask for your support to [modify the design of the project; implement traffic calming; protect our children from harmful chemicals; increase playing time and improve safety for our soccer teams . . .]."

This speaker is paving the way for the public official to vote yes and feel good about it, and for members of the community to join him. You may have very good reason to disdain your local public officials (I hope not, but there are some bad actors.) Deal with it later, not in public.

After the public meeting, you can vent to your friends. But if you want to use the public process to get something you want, you are more likely to succeed if you treat the process and its participants with respect. Also, remember, most public meetings are recorded and broadcast over local television channels or at least available after the fact on city websites. As they say, anything you say can and will be used against you if your opponents find it helpful. Being seen as nasty and emotional does not help your cause.

There is strength in numbers. It's always good to have allies, and being able to show decision-makers that your issue is a community issue, not just a personal preference, is important. Presenting a petition or asking people in the chamber to raise their hands or hold up a (small) sign to show their support when you speak can be very effective. Open meeting laws require governing bodies to allow the public to speak, normally with time limits of three to nine minutes. But you need to use good judgment in how many people take the microphone on behalf of your issue. Having a few diverse voices is good. Having dozens of speakers repeating the same points can be counterproductive and annoying.

Using Social Media

Another aspect of going public is using local news outlets and social media. There are many resources on how to effectively use social media. Here we cover a few ideas. The **Toolbox** ⟨ section on social media has more information and sample templates.

To get on an agenda: If you hit a brick wall entirely and see no movement to get your item on the agenda, try to find out who's blocking it. You can ask each council member directly and you might find an answer. If not, you might have to escalate your issue. So far, we have advised you to play nicely. Sometimes that's not enough. Try a letter to the editor or social media commentary.

To notify people: When there is a significant event happening, like a meeting of the planning commission or the city council when your item will be heard, let people know. You may need to do this using multiple methods which is time consuming. Not everyone reads email promptly. Not everyone has read this book and knows how to get notifications automatically.

Encourage supporters to spread the word using their social media and other networks. Council members notice when their inbox fills up with individually written (not generic) messages about an issue. Phone calls are also effective, but don't end up creating a public record.

Writing a letter to the editor or a slightly longer commentary in a local publication can also garner attention. Before the elected officials take action, your piece should make the case, using basically the same talking points you used when meeting with the decision-makers. Your goal is to convey that doing what you are asking will be good for the community and those who vote for it are heroes and deserve praise.

After action is taken--i.e., if you prevail--be sure to write something for publication thanking the council and applauding them for their concern for the community, their willingness to listen, their responsiveness, and so forth. Mention by name those who voted with you if the decision was not unanimous. You can try to get a letter to the editor, and you can also use your social media. A personal note written to each council member or commissioner is also very much appreciated and will put you in good stead the next time you want something done.

Before we see how Jacinta, Matt and Lee fared, the next chapter addresses what to do if these efforts don't bring satisfaction.

CHAPTER 7

WHAT NEXT?

Let's assume you have decided enough is enough. You've given your best effort and you have made a difference, regardless of the specific outcome. Every time a citizen exercises their right to engage in the governance process, they make a difference. Raising an issue, even if you don't prevail, has an impact. It might start the wheels moving in ways you don't realize. Maybe the second or third time someone brings up that problem, the council will decide it really does need attention. Maybe the next election will change who is on the dais and bring someone more sympathetic to your cause. Maybe you evolve in your understanding and redirect your energy in some way. We want to emphasize that government moves slowly and clumsily. But it does move. And it moves in response to public pressure. So, know that you are doing important work by getting educated and getting involved. Thank you.

Jacinta, Matt, and Lee

In our case, Jacinta, Matt, and Lee are not interested in pursuing legal action. Let's see what they have accomplished. Each of them got their issue in front of decision-makers who had the authority to take action. They activated other residents to pay attention to their issue and make their voices heard. Jacinta got the attention of the city leadership not just on her issue of pesticide use, but on the broader point that they have to look at what existing policies say and make sure they are following them. The city manager instructed every department head to review the sections of the municipal code and related policy documents in their area. If there are old regulations that no longer make sense, the city manager will bring a comprehensive list of updates to the city council with recommendations on which to keep, update, or drop. That's a big deal! Way to go, Jacinta.

As far as her actual proposal to ban pesticides, the council was undecided. They had heard some concerns about potential costs and a desire from residents to ensure that the parks were free from weeds and pests. After all, at a public hearing, the council will hear from all interested parties, not just you and your allies. No action was taken by the council the first time the agenda item was heard, other than to encourage the city manager to ensure that all landscape contractors were following approved procedures and reporting requirements.

Jacinta didn't give up. She met with the most supportive council member and together they came up with an incremental approach that the council member thought she could convince the others to approve--pick one park and do a one-year pilot project. Because of Jacinta's advocacy the council member worked with city staff to define what that would look like.

Staff said they could figure out how much the city was spending now for landscaping and treatments and take pictures and document the condition of the trees and other plants. With council approval, they would adopt the most current organic landscape practices for that park and keep careful records on costs and conditions. Then staff would report back to the council after a year and hope that they have demonstrated that this would be a good approach for all public spaces. The council member talked to the city manager and the parks department director and got their confirmation that this was possible--they had the data and personnel to do a pilot project and it seemed they were enthusiastic about the idea.

The council member and Jacinta decided it would be best if Jacinta proposed the idea at a council meeting and the council member could be ready to push for council approval. Jacinta went back and met with all the other council members individually to let them know what she was proposing. They all thought it sounded reasonable.

In addition, they appreciated not being taken by surprise in public as would have happened if she had proposed it at a meeting without talking to them first. Jacinta spoke at another council meeting during the general comment period and asked for her pilot project idea to be put on a future agenda. Her ally on the council spoke in support and the other council members, who had already been briefed on the idea, agreed. A few weeks later, the pilot project was unanimously approved.

Matt is making progress, as the housing project he's concerned with moves through the approval process. He spoke in front of the planning commission about saving the trees and about design guidelines. He was assured that in the environmental review for the project, the city would include a provision to save as many trees as possible. He was told how to track the project and where to find reports on landscape plans where the developer has to submit reports about any trees they think need to be removed.

Matt will have to wait for those reports to know whether his concerns have been met. At least he is on record and knows what to expect next. He also learns when in the process the exterior design features will be reviewed so he can participate in that public hearing. The planning staff has a special email notification list for people interested in this specific project, and Matt's name is now on that list, so he is recognized as an interested party. It's a long process and patience and persistence are required. Decision-makers have been alerted to your issues, and that's progress. Don't give up now, Matt.

Lee has learned a lot. She has learned that infrastructure projects, even small ones, take money, time and persistence. 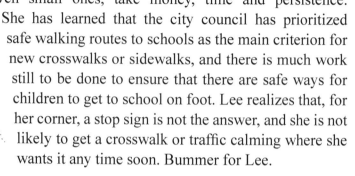 She has learned that the city council has prioritized safe walking routes to schools as the main criterion for new crosswalks or sidewalks, and there is much work still to be done to ensure that there are safe ways for children to get to school on foot. Lee realizes that, for her corner, a stop sign is not the answer, and she is not likely to get a crosswalk or traffic calming where she wants it any time soon. Bummer for Lee.

She also recognizes that having safe ways for kids to get to and from school is more important, and she appreciates that the city has established that priority. Lee decides that walking a few extra blocks to get to an existing stoplight where she can safely cross with her dog is the best way to ensure their safe route to the park. She feels disappointed but accepting, and she is much more informed. She is now one of the advocates for increasing funding for school-related sidewalk improvements.

Other Options

So here we are. Some of you may have found satisfaction in your efforts. Others may not yet be ready to move on. Here are some other ideas to consider. Maybe in the end, you need to take a broader view and form or join a non-governmental organization (NGO) that is working on the bigger issues that encompass your concerns. Maybe you conclude that the only way to change the system enough to make a difference is for you to run for public office, whether at the local, state, or national level. Maybe you want to get involved in politics behind the scene and work to influence current officeholders and candidates running for office.

You have many avenues open for active participation. Each has costs--financial, emotional, and social. Only you can determine the right course of action for you.

CLOSING THOUGHTS

Whatever the outcome of your efforts, it is likely that you will be paying more attention now to what's happening in your community. Every time you see city workers performing maintenance in a park, or signs announcing a new development, you will realize what it took for that to happen. We get the kind of government we choose, either by our participation or our disengagement.

Government works slowly, by design. It doesn't take rocket science, but it does take patience. The public participation process is cumbersome and frustrating. Open government rules mean that we have to slow down enough for people to engage in the process. We have a complex web of overlapping and interdependent jurisdictions, and a collection of elected officials worrying about reelection, overseeing professional staff, often with more experience and expertise. And we have residents who have a wide range of priorities and preferences. But hang in there. Individual efforts can make a difference and often transform the outcome.

The authors, one who served for eight years and the other for four, did make a meaningful difference in our community, in part because of the efforts of ordinary citizens who educated us, allied with us, and pushed us. Our efforts were also informed by our own experiences prior to election, trying to have a voice as a member of the public. One of our proudest achievements was to make the city's decision-making process more accessible and less intimidating, in response to the frustration we and others felt as ordinary community members trying to be heard. Some of the things that were accomplished while we were in office include:

Process Improvements

- Made it easier for council members to add items to future agendas
- Reformed public commissions, including term limits
- Introduced use of online civic engagement platform to increase public participation
- Expanded public notification about closed sessions so people know what is being discussed.
- Added an option to the public comment process to enable people to choose "support but do not wish to speak" or "oppose but do not wish to speak"

Policy Changes

- Banned single-use plastic bags
- Created a budget process to pay down unfunded pension liabilities
- Increased fees from developers going toward affordable housing
- Updated and adopted new policies on urban forests, small-scale agriculture in residential zones, and pesticide-free parks
- Approved creation of first community garden

Public Investments

- Purchased an abandoned public school property to maintain open, public space downtown and provide for future use as an arts and ecology education center
- Funded and approved new marine safety center
- Increased funding for road maintenance
- Enabled creation of affordable housing project

We both believe deeply in good government and the importance of public education and engagement. We didn't always have fun, but we always felt satisfied that we were doing our part to create the kind of community and society we value. You can too.

SECTION 2

SECTION 2

DIGGING DEEPER

Levels of Government

People living in the United States are subject to laws at the federal, state, and local government level, starting with the US Constitution. There is no mention in the constitution of city or county governments. They derive their authority from their individual states. As the National League of Cities says, "It is not surprising, then, that there is a great diversity in state-local relations between, as well as within, states. This means that to speak of local government in the United States is to speak of more than fifty different legal and political situations."[4]

Furthermore, there is a court ruling called "Dillon's Rule" that says that municipal governments can only exercise powers granted to them by the state. State constitutions vary in the level of power they grant to local governments.

It is impractical to describe here, in any complete sense, what authority city governments have. However, there are some general facts we can provide. Local governments typically come in these forms:

- "Counties. Counties are usually the largest political subdivisions, and their primary function is to administer state laws within their borders. Among other duties, they keep the peace, maintain jails, collect taxes, build and repair roads and bridges, and record deeds, marriages, and deaths. Elected officials called supervisors or commissioners usually lead counties.

- Townships. These units of government do not exist in about half the states, and they have different responsibilities in those that have them. A township may simply be another name for a town or city, or it may be a subdivision of a county.

- Special Districts. These units of government have special functions. The best-known example is the local school district, but other types are growing in numbers, especially in heavily populated areas where county and city governments may be overloaded with work.

- Municipalities. City, town, or borough governments get their authority to rule only as it is granted by the state. Today about 80 percent of the American population lives in municipalities, and municipal governments affect the lives of many citizens. Municipalities may have elected mayors, or they may be managed by appointed city managers."[5]

Who Does What?

In a city manager/city council form of government, the city council only has authority to hire and fire the city manager and city attorney. All other personnel actions are the city manager's responsibility. This is designed to protect the staff from pressure to play favorites or take actions that don't reflect the formal direction from the council majority. In a strong mayor city, senior staff report directly to the mayor.

Mayors do not all have the same authority-- it depends on the form of government. Generally speaking, mayoral responsibilities may include:

- Serving on the city council;
- Setting council meeting agenda;
- Voting in council meetings;
- Assigning council members to chair or serve on committees;
- Appointing citizens to serve on advisory boards or commissions;
- Preparing the annual budget; Receiving the annual budget developed by chief administrative official or city manager; and
- Making an annual report to the council.

Cities may have a strong or weak mayor--a description of the mayor's authority, not their competence. From the League of Cities[6], here is an explanation:

Characteristics of a "strong" mayor:

- The mayor is the chief executive officer, centralizing executive power.
- The mayor directs the administrative structure, appointing and removing department heads.
- While the council has legislative power, the mayor has veto power.
- The council does not oversee daily operations.

Characteristics of a "weak" mayor:

- The council is powerful, with both legislative and executive authority.
- The mayor is not truly the chief executive, with limited power or no veto power.
- The council can prevent the mayor from effectively supervising city administration.
- There may be many administrative boards and commissions that operate independently from the city government.

To make things more complicated, consider this. Two states have eliminated counties altogether; in other states counties may contain cities within them; others provide the functions of both a county and a city. For example, Arlington, Virginia, just outside of Washington, DC, is a county without any associated city governments. The county is managed by an elected board, one member of which serves as its chair. The board hires a county manager. Within the county, there is a school board and a judicial system. The county government has departments addressing public health; environmental services; planning, housing, and development; and public safety, among others.

In addition, Arlington County participates in broader regional planning groups that oversee some aspects of the greater Washington, DC metropolitan area, such as " the Metropolitan Washington Council of Governments. This agency consists of twenty-two local jurisdictions, including the county, with a mission to enhance the quality of life and competitive advantages of the Washington metropolitan region in a number of areas such as transportation and the environment."[7]

In San Diego, the county includes eighteen incorporated cities and unincorporated areas. The County Board of Supervisors provides direct authority over the unincorporated areas and shares power with the city councils of the incorporated cities. The San Diego Association of Governments (SANDAG) is that county's regional planning board, comprising elected officials from the cities and the county. SANDAG's website defines its role as "the forum for regional decision-making." SANDAG manages transportation planning and consolidates funding from regional taxes and grants from state and federal agencies to build projects in the region and provide funding to cities for local projects. Nothing is simple!

Money, Money, Money

Because each state and region may have different governmental arrangements, it's hard to generalize about funding and budgets. Typically, local governments are largely funded by property taxes, and many also receive sales tax revenue (whether a specific local sales tax or a formula-based share of state sales tax). Cities may receive grants from state and federal agencies. There is also income from license fees such as required for business permits and fees from recreational programs. The chart below is an aggregate representation of California cities' income and expenditures.[8]

Discretionary Revenues and Spending
Typical Full Service City

Often, infrastructure projects such as roads, bridges, and transit systems are funded by a combination of federal, state, and local sources, with each level of government imposing standards that must be met to qualify for the funding. At the city level, decisions involve which projects to propose, where to seek funding, and how to balance local control with external requirements from funders. Similarly, education is typically "controlled" by a local school board but in order to qualify for federal funds in specific areas, the school must meet requirements set in Washington.

Budgets and the Power of Cities

The process of developing a city's budget varies--it may be prepared by the mayor, by the city manager and staff, or through some other arrangement. No matter how the proposed budget is created, the city council has the sole authority for approving the budget through passage of a budget ordinance, and any changes to it will also require council approval.

Most states also require cities to maintain a balanced budget, so municipal budgets typically include substantial reserves to accommodate unexpected events.

A longtime city manager said her two most frequently heard comments were "I pay your salary" (and so you have to do what I'm asking) and "Do you know how much I pay in property taxes to fund this city?" (so you have to do what I'm asking). This is not a winning strategy. It may be helpful to understand where your city's funding comes from.

Cities, counties, and states vary in using their powers. Each may impose taxes (normally subject to a public vote) but not all do so. For example, Alaska, Tennessee, Wyoming and Florida have no state income tax. There are over eleven thousand sales tax jurisdictions in the United States, with widely varying rates. Among major cities, Chicago, Illinois and Long Beach and Glendale, California impose the highest combined state and local sales tax rates, at 10.25 percent. . . . Neither Anchorage, Alaska, nor Portland, Oregon, impose any state or local sales taxes.[9]

The importance of property taxes in city governments varies widely, depending on what other revenue sources are available. States may have state income taxes, sales taxes, or other taxes and fees. Some cities have their own sales or income tax requirements, as well as special fees like hotel/tourism assessments. How revenues from these sources are allocated to the state government, cities, and other entities like school districts and special districts also varies, even within a state. In California, for example, when a city is incorporated, the state negotiates a formula for sharing property taxes. Our city gets $0.24 of each dollar of property tax. A smaller, older neighboring city gets only $0.10/dollar.

The figure below shows the relative importance of property tax revenue in each state.[10]

FIGURE 1
Property Tax Revenue as a Percentage of State and Local Own-Source General Revenue
2016

Source: Urban-Brookings Tax Policy Center, "State and Local Finance Initiative, Data Query System."
Note: Own-source general revenue does not include intergovernmental transfers.

General Plans

In doing your homework, you may hear reference to the General Plan, sometimes called a Comprehensive Plan or Master Plan. The requirements for cities to adopt and maintain updated general plans varies from state to state--in some states it is mandatory, in others it is recommended. If your city has a General Plan, it will consist of sections called "elements." General plans typically cover a ten-year period and provide the high-level framework for planning decisions. Where such plans have been adopted, specific regulations and actions must be consistent with the general plan. For example, the Institute for Local Government describes the situation in California:

"California law requires each city and county within the state to adopt 'a comprehensive, long-term general plan for the physical development' of the land within its present and likely future boundaries. All other land use regulations and decisions within the jurisdiction must conform to the general plan. For example, if the general plan identifies community gardens as a priority use for vacant lots in residential neighborhoods, zoning cannot prohibit this use. If the zoning code does not allow community gardens, then it must be amended to be consistent with the general plan.

The components of a general plan are called elements. There are seven elements required by the state. (State law does permit the combining of elements.) A jurisdiction may have as many elements as it chooses--so long as it has the mandatory seven, which are:

- Land Use: Designates the general location and intensity of housing, business, industry, open space, education, public buildings and grounds, waste disposal facilities, and other land uses.
- Circulation: Identifies the general location and extent of

existing and proposed major roads, transportation routes, bicycle routes, walking trails, terminals, and public utilities and facilities. Like all other elements, it must be consistent with the land use element.

• Housing: Involves a comprehensive assessment of current and projected housing needs for all economic segments of the community and region. It sets forth local housing policies and programs to implement those policies.

• Conservation: Addresses the conservation, development, and use of natural resources including water, forests, soils, rivers, and mineral deposits.

• Open Space: Details plans and measures for preserving open space for natural resources, the managed production of resources, outdoor recreation, public health and safety, and the identification of agricultural land.

• Noise: Identifies and appraises noise problems within the community and forms the basis for distributing new noise-sensitive land uses.

• Safety: Establishes policies and programs to protect the community from risks associated with seismic, geologic, flood, and wildfire hazards."[11]

This document below is from the Colorado Department of Local Affairs, describing what they call a Master Plan. Unlike California where a city council must enact the general plan, in Colorado, the plan is adopted by the planning commission.

STATE OF COLORADO
DEPARTMENT OF LOCAL AFFAIRS

MASTER PLAN PRIMER

MASTER PLAN – GENERAL DESCRIPTION
The master plan, sometimes referred to as a comprehensive plan, is a framework and guide for accomplishing community aspirations and intentions. It states goals and objectives and recommends courses of action for future growth and development of land, public facilities and services and environmental protection.

PLAN ELEMENTS THAT MAY BE INCLUDED

- Statement of Objectives, Policies and Programs
- Relationship of Plan to the Trends/Plans of the Region
- Land Use
- Transportation
- Utility and Facility Plan

- Urban Influence Area
- Housing
- Cultural/Historical/Social Setting
- Educational Facilities
- Energy
- Environment
- Recreation and Tourism*

*the only plan element required by statutes (see C.R.S. 30-28-106 and 31-23-206)

BASIS/BACKGROUND FOR PLAN INFORMATION
The plan is based on inventories, studies, surveys, analysis of current trends and must consider social and economic consequences of the plan and existing and projected population.

GOALS AND OBJECTIVES OF THE PLAN
The principal purpose for a master plan is to be a guide for the achievement of community goals. A plan will also:

1. State and promote broad community values in the plan goals, objectives, policies and programs.
2. Establish a planning process for orderly growth and development, and economic health.
3. Balance competing interests and demands.
4. Provide for coordination and coherence in the pattern of development.
5. Provide for a balance between the natural and built environment.
6. Reflect regional conditions and consider regional impacts.
7. Address both current and long-term needs.

It is used as described here:

USING THE PLAN

The adopted plan has the potential for many uses and will define the way it is to be used in its implementation section. Among the uses of the plan are the following:

1. A basis for Regulatory Actions: The plan serves as a foundation guide for the provisions of the zoning regulations, subdivision regulations, the land use map, flood hazard regulations, annexation decisions and other decisions made under these regulations.

2. A basis for community programs and Decision Making: The plan is a guide and resource for the recommendations contained in a capital budget and program, for a community development program, and for direction and content of other local initiatives, such as water protection, recreation or open space land acquisition and housing.

3. A source for planning studies: Few plans can address every issue in sufficient detail. Therefore, many plans will recommend further studies to develop courses of action on a specific need.

4. A standard for review at the County and State level: Other regulatory processes identify the municipal plan as a standard for review of applications. Master plans are important to the development of regional plans or inter- municipal programs, i.e., a regional trail network or area transit program.

5. A source of information: The plan is a valuable source of information for local boards, commissions, organizations, citizens and business.

6. A long-term guide: The plan is a long-term guide by which to measure and evaluate public and private proposals that affect the physical, social, and economic environment of the community."[12]

You can see that there is a great deal of similarity across states. While not all issues rise to the level of conformance with the general plan, it is good to look at the elements relevant to your interests and be able to relate your concerns to stated goals or policies in your locality's master plan.

Do You Need a Lawyer?

Here, we are not talking about what happens if a city truck backs into your parked car, or if a defective piece of playground equipment

The authors are not lawyers and this section (and the whole book) should not be taken as legal advice.

results in personal injury. These are matters where either the city takes responsibility and works out a mutually acceptable resolution, or you might sue for restitution. This section explores how or when you might use the court system to address compliance in an area where the city has a mandated responsibility to do or not do something, for example, issues like zoning approvals or stormwater discharge regulations. We also note that for some issues, there are other channels in which to pursue remedies, such as the city's code enforcement staff or an appeal to a higher-level organization like a regional or state commission.

If you decide to consult a lawyer, choose carefully. Your brother-in-law's friend who specializes in estate law is not likely to be of much help. Attorneys who have experience in your community, and in your area of interest can be invaluable.

Depending on their experience and reputation, just knowing they are involved can influence the process. In fact, it might just take one phone call for a local legal expert to tell you what you can realistically expect about a particular project, based on the attorney's knowledge of laws, the applicable municipal code or regulations, past cases, the staff and the other parties involved. They can also help you find information and build your case. A good attorney will also tell you when their services are not needed, either because the issue is straightforward or because you have unrealistic expectations and no chance of success.

If you choose to use a lawyer, gather as many facts as you can, but don't spend a lot of time trying to become a legal expert--that's why you're asking a lawyer. Use the lawyer for their expertise. Then you can save money by doing research and having factual information well organized, so you don't have to pay the law firm for research you could do yourself. In addition to finding someone with the relevant expertise, it is important that you feel comfortable communicating with the attorney--the better your communication, the better you can work together on your issue.

The authors spoke to several attorneys who work on local issues, and they all said that in at least half of the initial consultations with prospective clients, the clients learn that they have no legal basis for what they were hoping to achieve.

Hiring a lawyer early in the process may help your chances of getting what you want without having to go to court. If you are not successful or satisfied, when all else fails, you may decide to resort to judicial action, suing the city government, to get what you're asking for.

"Virtually every reference guide on Municipal Law begins with the premise that a city has the police power to protect the public health, safety and welfare of its residents. . . . This right is set forth in the California Constitution, which states 'A county or city may make and enforce within its limits all local, police, sanitary, and other ordinances and regulations not in conflict with general laws.'" [13] These police powers are the source of city authority to establish land use and zoning laws which govern the development and use of the community.

In land use cases, typically the planning commission has the authority to approve or disapprove a project. These decisions can be appealed to the city council or county board. The elected body has the final authority. The municipal code typically lays out the appeal procedures, including timelines. Appeals must specify the grounds on which the appellant is asking for a different decision.

If you believe that the city is not complying with an existing law, whether that is a federal, state, or local law, and you have not been able to persuade the city to come into compliance, you can file a lawsuit. Approval of new development projects often attract lawsuits because the policies and procedures are complex and subject to interpretation. Unhappy residents can challenge the outcome by looking for process errors. Examples of process errors could be improper posting of public hearings, or inadequate or erroneous studies (traffic, environment, etc.) used to support a project.

You may choose to use the courts if you see your city violating environmental regulations--for example not managing stormwater runoff on a public construction site, or in states with mandatory greenhouse gas emission reduction standards, your city's emissions are too high.

One of the first questions to ask is whether you have "standing" or a legal right to bring a lawsuit on the particular issue. Property owners have the right to develop their property if they conform to applicable rules and regulations. If the city followed the right procedures and you just don't like the outcome, you probably cannot win a lawsuit. Your initial consultation with an attorney should reveal whether or not you have the basis for moving forward in the legal system.

Don't believe any attorney who says a win is a sure thing. There are no sure things. Judges, just like city council members and staff, make mistakes and have biases. Also don't believe an attorney who says it's simple or quick. Land use cases can sometimes drag out over years, many years. The first development appeal that Lisa had to vote on was not finally resolved for seven years from when the planning commission first heard it.

Money, Money, Money

Generally, in our legal system, each side pays its own legal fees. However, there are statutes that allow, in some cases, for a private party to recover attorney's fees from a government entity if the private party prevails. The reverse does not apply--private parties will not be required to pay the government's legal expenses. What is sometimes overlooked is that when you sue your city government, you are suing yourself and your neighbors. Legal expenses for government entities typically are paid out of the general budget, at the expense of other things the city might have done with those funds. Just something to think about.

Attorneys use different fee structures. For some cases, you may pay a straight hourly rate. Some cases are significant enough to the attorney that they will work pro bono or on a contingency basis, taking their fees out of the settlement if their side prevails and the court awards legal fees to be paid by the government.

Winning Isn't Everything

Some other things to think about: a good attorney may be able to find a technicality on which to base a lawsuit and overturn a decision-- you may be concerned about traffic impacts from a housing project, but the attorney finds a flaw in the air quality analysis and uses that as leverage to sue, and a court agrees. The remedy, however, may not be to stop the project. It may be that the city has to go back and reevaluate the air quality study; the applicant may have to do additional mitigation. The project may end up proceeding with the same traffic impacts that caused you to sue in the first place.

On the other hand, sometimes a lawsuit or just the threat of a lawsuit, especially if your attorney has a certain reputation, can be enough to scuttle a project. Time is money, as they say, and anticipating a long, drawn out battle may cause a developer who hasn't yet finalized a possible development to decide to look elsewhere to build.

If your real issue, when you really probe your own motivations, is an attempt to stop time, to turn back development, to keep your town the cozy little burg that it was when your grandparents moved there, you may be frustrated even if you manage to stop a particular project. Before undertaking the expense, stress, and uncertainty of litigation, consider whether a legal victory will really satisfy what is really bothering you.

SECTION 3

SECTION 3

TOOLBOX

This section contains the tools you will need to get something done. They say, "measure twice, cut once." This is good advice for advocates, too. Make sure you know what you're doing before picking up the sledgehammer. Perhaps a gentle tap or tightening a loose connector is all that's really needed.

The first step in doing your homework is to get the basic facts in hand. Here are questions you should be able to answer before taking any action.

- In what city does your problem occur?

- What form of government does your city have?

- Who is the mayor? Who is on the city council?

- Who represents you, where you live? Is it the same person who represents the location where your issue arises?

- What public commissions are in your city (e.g., planning, parks, traffic)?

- Who represents you on the commission that relates to your issue?

- Who is the city manager?

- What information is on the city's website?

Once you have the basic information in hand, you can move on to defining your problem. Think carefully and use this worksheet to help you clarify what you're really trying to achieve.

Problem Worksheet

When you decide it's time for action, this worksheet may help you plan your moves. Later you will convert this into your case statement.

1. What is the issue?

In a nutshell, why are you doing this? What's the "WHY" that motivates you? If your mother-in-law or your partner asks you why you're spending time on this project, do you have a short, simple answer? Be sure to describe the problem, not yet the solution.

In our examples, Jacinta's problem is landscape contractors spraying pesticides. Matt's issue is a new higher density housing project. Lee's issue is an unsafe intersection between her and a park.

2. What is the goal?

This is where some introspection is needed. In our examples, Jacinta would say her goal is safe outdoor public spaces. Matt might say "stop the housing project" but as we see, the real issue is probably something else--protect property values or avoid traffic congestion or save old trees. Lee wants to be able to get her dog to the park safely on foot. One way to think about this is to ask what would have to happen for you to feel satisfied and go home.

3. Who has the authority? City, state, county, school board, and so on. . . . Who specifically--city council, city manager, fire chief, school board. . . .?

This section may require some research. The answer may not be clear due to overlapping jurisdictions. If you can't find the answer on your own or through the magic of internet searching, contact the entity you think has authority and ask. Remember, these folks work for you and part of their job is answering questions from the public they serve.

4. What don't you know that you can find out? Is there existing law? If so, does it need to be amended or just enforced? Does new law or regulation need to be developed? As much as possible, can you find out why things are the way they are today. You may find that what you want just isn't legal and based on past deliberations or court cases, will never be allowed. Sorry.

5. Is your issue broadly focused or likely to only be of interest to a small number of residents?

6. What possible solutions have you identified?

7. What resources might be needed (budget, personnel) and are there offsetting revenue opportunities?

You are not likely to be an expert on your city's budget, but most cities put their financial information online. You could see if there is a line item for landscape maintenance or for traffic calming. If you are proposing a new program that will require staff, are there examples of the city collecting fees that cover some of the costs? Can you make the case that your project is a higher priority than others that are listed in the budget? You may not be able to figure out all the answers but being aware that your ideas might have resource impacts should help you frame your expectations realistically.

8. Other stakeholders--who else cares or should care about your issue?

9. Are there examples from other cities that might help inform your efforts? This could either be successes or failures--either way, how could your city learn from the experiences of others?

Finding Information

Online Resources

Background information about local topics is found in many places, from the local public library and newspaper archives to research papers at think tanks or advocacy organizations. If you are interested in transportation planning, for example, the Institute of Traffic Engineers has a technical resource page[14] with reports on transportation issues. The US Environmental Protection Agency provides information on pesticides[15]. Local nonprofits, like San Diego's Community Housing Works[16], and industry groups like the California Building Industries Association[17] (there is a chapter in every state), have resources about housing. Most states will also have a Department of Housing such as the https://www.hcd.ca.gov/. As with any research effort, you need to be conscious of any potential biases in the information presented and try to find multiple sources to get background material that is as complete and objective as possible.

Within your local jurisdiction, the city government is the best place to understand what laws and regulations already exist, related to your issue. Don't be afraid to ask what you think may be "dumb questions." The only dumb questions are the ones you wish you had asked but were afraid to. Your tax dollars pay the salaries of the people working in your city hall, and generally speaking, they know that they work for you. If you are reasonable and respectful, you can get a lot of help at city hall.

Many cities provide online access to their municipal code, i.e., local laws. The municipal code, as defined by the Library of Congress, is "the collection of laws passed by a local governing body (often of a county, city, village, township, or other similar governmental subdivision). The laws themselves can be referred to by many names, including 'ordinance,' 'bylaw,' and 'measure,' among others. As long as they do not conflict with the laws of the state in which the municipality is located, these ordinances have the 'force and effect of law' in the municipality."[18]

If someone tells you that they don't have to do something because it's just the municipal code, not the law, you need to know that the municipal code IS the law.

The town of Pittsford, New York has its code online. Here is a sample page:

City Clerk

If you can't find the municipal code, or if your attempts at deciphering the sometimes-arcane language of the code are unsuccessful, the next stop could be the city clerk. According to the City Clerks Association of California,

"The Office of the City Clerk is a service department within the municipal government upon which the City Council, all City departments, and the general public rely for information regarding the operations and legislative history of the City. The City Clerk serves *as the liaison between the public and City Council* and provides related municipal services. ...As a Records Manager, the City Clerk oversees yet another legislative process; the preservation and protection of the public record. By statute, the City Clerk is required to maintain and index the Minutes, Ordinances, and Resolutions adopted by the legislative body. The City Clerk also ensures that other municipal records are readily accessible to the public."[19]

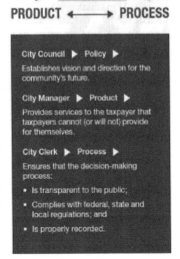

As with any interaction, it helps to be prepared and clear when asking for the city clerk's help. But don't hesitate to ask. It is the clerk's job to make sure that the public can find out what is going on and what has already happened. The illustration[20] shows the roles of the city council (setting policy), the city manager/staff (implementing policies), and the city clerk (managing the process).

Public Record Request

If a simple request to an elected official or city staff person does not provide the information you are seeking, in most cases you can obtain it through a public records request. Each state has its own rules but in general, non-sensitive information must be provided upon request. Your request should describe what you're looking for in as much specificity as possible--e.g., all emails and written correspondence from January 1, 2020 to March 31, 2020, to or from any elected official or city staff member regarding pesticides. You may be asked to specify whether you want a paper copy or an electronic file. There may be fees associated with records requests. There may be statutory deadlines for replies.

The National Freedom of Information Coalition has conducted six biennial open government surveys. The survey's purpose "is to identify current trends in public institutions for requesting and accessing public records. This survey provides important information suggesting needed reforms to improve public information management and access in state and local government."[21]

Among their findings:

- "Nearly 87% of respondents said the incidence of open records or open meeting violations in their state and local jurisdiction stayed steady or increased over the past two years.
- More than half of respondents said government officials' understanding of and voluntary compliance with open government requirements in their state and local jurisdiction decreased over the past two years.
- Reported reasons for government agencies denying access to records varied, from disingenuous rationalization of exemptions to inappropriate game playing and ignorance

of the law. The biggest obstacle respondents said they faced in getting information was a lack of response or delayed response (84%), followed by invalid exceptions (66%) and unreasonable fees (63%).

- 21% of respondents said there were worse policy reforms, amendments and legislative changes to public disclosure and open meeting laws affecting their state; 15% said it had improved.

- As in past surveys, state and local law enforcement agencies continue to be the most challenging among government agencies to obtain public records (58.5%) according to the respondents."

At the local level, issues like data retention policies may inhibit public records requests--if someone has deleted their emails or erased phone messages, there is no record. Issues arise, as we have seen at the national level, about use of personal devices and accounts instead of official ones. Some public officials are more careful than others about putting anything in writing, largely because of public records requests. Unfortunately, many important discussions take place in person or over the phone just to avoid the creation of a record that might be requested in the future.

The Center's website[22] can take you to your state's public records laws and provide sample request templates. If you don't find your city's code on the city's website, there are online databases such as Municode[23] with the municipal codes of many cities.

Ideally, the information will be searchable, and you can enter a few key words and see what comes up. Sometimes you will be surprised by what is in your city's legal system. For example, while searching for something else, I came across section 9.24.010 in the Encinitas municipal code that states it is "unlawful to appear, bathe, sunbathe, walk or be in any public place, which includes being on public or private property in a location open to public view from adjacent public or private property in such a manner that the . . . natal cleft . . . of any person . . . is exposed to public view or is not covered by an opaque covering.[24] You'll have to look that one up. Hint: plumbing contractors, beware!!

How to Talk to Staff

You can only do your part: being respectful of their time and expertise; being open to listening as well as talking; and trying to find common ground so you can fix the problem that brought you there. Remember: civility, clarity, and communication. Whether or not you have a theory about why things are the way they are, it's a good idea to ask open-ended questions of staff and try to elicit their perspective. Here are some sample questions you could ask:

- Tell me about [the rules for landscape contractors using pesticides; the new housing project; how you are reducing pedestrian accidents at my corner; . . .]

- How do you decide [which contractors; what products are used; where to build; which intersections to focus on . . .]

- Who has the authority to make those decisions?

- When and why were those policies/laws enacted?

- Has anyone tried to [ban pesticides; stop the project; add more stop signs; . . .] What happened?

- What would be needed to make the change I'm talking about?

Even if you have asked the same question of others, it's useful to see whether all the key players have the same understanding and outlook.

Sample Case Statement: Turf for the Soccer Field

SUMMARY

We request that the city council replace the existing grass at the soccer field in Pele Park with CocoTurf or another eco-friendly surface. Approximately X days/year, our one municipal soccer field is not available for use due to maintenance requirements. Another Y days/year it is unusable because it is too muddy after a rain. Replacing the grass with eco-friendly artificial turf would make the field safer, more usable, and reduce maintenance costs. This proposal is supported by the majority of families with players in the recreational and travel soccer teams.

WHY THIS, WHY NOW?

Soccer is the most popular recreational and league sport for students in our town. Players have had to travel to other cities to find available practice fields and to participate in tournaments because our local field is out of commission so often. Recent studies have shown that, unlike earlier rubber-based artificial surfaces, natural fiber turf is now available and can safely replace natural grass. [include reference to these studies]

In addition, the water district is offering rebates for removing grass and permanently reducing water demand. Switching from grass to artificial turf reduces water use by X percent and the city may qualify for a rebate to offset some of the initial costs. The deadline for rebates is [date].

WHO WOULD HAVE TO DO WHAT?

The city owns Pele Park and the Parks & Recreation Department manages it. *We have identified three companies that provide safe products using coconut fiber. In fact, one of our soccer parents works for CocoTurf and might be able to get us a special deal.* **[RED FLAG: Do not mix business with politics--avoid anything that looks like a conflict of interest. How do decision-makers know that you are advocating for the best solution objectively, or just trying to steer business to someone in the soccer club? There is a line between being helpful and inappropriately trying to control a public process.]** Instead, try this: We are confident that there are multiple suppliers and the city will be able to choose one through a competitive process.

There will be an upfront investment of approximately $$ required, based on an average cost of $X/square foot reported by other cities, and annual maintenance costs of $ABC. We were unable to separate the city's annual maintenance cost just for Pele Park from the overall park maintenance budget line. But we believe that the eco-turf investment will pay back in just a few years and make our kids more competitive and safer. In addition, the water department rebate could offset some of the initial costs, and the reduced need to water the field will provide savings in water usage.

[NOTE: Ideally, you could provide an apples-to-apples cost comparison but this is really something the staff would have to do anyway in preparation for presenting anything to the council.]

We have reviewed the city's general plan, and the parks and recreation element says the city shall "provide the playing fields necessary to serve the community," but does not establish any specific standards for "special use parks" which is what Pele Park is.

WHO ARE THE STAKEHOLDERS?

An overwhelming majority of soccer families support this proposal. We have a petition signed by XXX families that we can present to the city. We can't think of anyone who would object. **[RED FLAG: There is always someone who would object. Unless there is an iron-clad guarantee that this solution will be less expensive, there will be people who object on fiscal grounds. There may be people who are nostalgic for grass and remember their childhoods and want to keep things "natural." There may also be skeptics about how safe eco-turf is. There will also be people who have other "pet projects" that they think should be higher priority. Be sure you have as much solid information as possible to respond to these potential challenges.]**

IS THERE A WIN-WIN?

This project should be supported by environmentalists concerned about water conservation. It should be supported by people concerned with children and public health--making it easier and safer for kids to play competitive sports outdoors. It should be supported by people concerned about fiscal responsibility because it will pay for itself in the long run. We can rally the soccer families to write letters, to speak at council meetings, and to support decision-makers who support us.

Two nearby cities have already made the switch to eco-turf. We understand that two others are considering it. Perhaps our city could work with them to get a better deal for three fields.

Talking One-on-One with Public Officials

It is important that you try to meet with all members of the commission, city council or county board, not just the ones you think will be supportive. In fact, the most important meetings are those with potential opponents. You should not assume you know how any elected official might vote, and you should not write off anyone without at least trying to persuade them to support you.

Nobody likes to look stupid, especially in public. Chances are that any given decision-maker has not studied every issue and does not understand deeply every aspect of municipal government. Individual meetings with decision-makers gives them a chance to ask questions and consider your ideas out of the public eye. If you present an issue, especially if it's complicated or esoteric, at a public meeting and it's the first time they have heard about it, they may be reluctant to admit their ignorance or seek enough information to make a good decision and tend to just say no. Also, you have a stronger case, if you end up speaking at a public meeting, if you can say that you met or tried to meet with all of them to ensure they had all the relevant background information.

Some will be cautious and not give any indication of their views, but others may be very open, expressing support or opposition. If they are already on board, use this occasion to thank them, and ask if there's anything else they need in terms of information or outreach. If they are opposed, ask why. Don't debate. Always have something to leave with them - it could be a one-page summary of your case statement with the key points, or a brochure, or your business card with a website address. When you get home, be sure to send an email or handwritten note thanking them again, and briefly reiterating your "ask."

Here is a sample thank-you note to send after meeting with a council member:

> Dear Councilmember Kabir:
>
> Thank you for meeting with me as a representative of the two-hundred-family Everytown Soccer League this afternoon to discuss the possibility of putting artificial turf on the community park soccer field. I appreciate your recognition that our kids will have more playing time and fewer injuries if we replace the old dirt and grass with environmentally friendly, safe Coco-Turf. As I indicated, the cost calculations show that after only two years, the city's investment will be recovered in savings compared to maintaining the existing grass. I will be sure to send you more details on the financial analysis as you requested. Feel free to contact me if you have any questions.

After your meetings, try to figure out what you can learn from their position. Do they have information you weren't aware of? Is there a problem with your proposal that you hadn't considered? Might they be flexible if they heard the message from a different constituent (i.e., do they associate you with their political opposition)? However the conversation goes, be sure to thank them for their time and consideration.

After trying to meet with all the decision-makers, you should have an idea of your chances.

> NOTE: If you discover that, despite your background research, your local government does not have the authority to take the action you want, but it's really a regional or state-level issue, you will need to shift your attention to the decision-makers

there. However, your work at the local level is not wasted--ask your elected officials to weigh in, to send a letter of support, or perhaps to make an introduction to help your case.

Speaking at a Public Meeting

An excerpt from a website of Middletown, New Jersey, describes the process for public speakers.[25]

Helpful Guide to a Township Committee Meeting

While attending a Township Committee meeting in Middletown, the following information may be helpful:

The Mayor is the chairperson for the meeting and appointed to that position by the other members of the Committee annually. The Deputy Mayor, or Vice Chairman, assumes the chair in the absence of the Mayor.

At every meeting, an Agenda is made available to the public to announce what items of business are before the Township Committee, and determine the flow of the meeting. The Township Committee conducts an agenda meeting which is a workshop session on the first Monday of every month to discuss items which will be acted upon at the next meeting unless otherwise posted.

Public participation is allowed during the public portion. Members of the public desiring to speak, must give their name and address and limit their statement to five minutes allowing for other members of the public to have a chance to speak.

Copies of the agenda for each of the meetings are available at all meetings and online at www.middletownnj.org the Friday before the regularly scheduled meeting. Copies of ordinances which will have their public hearings are also available to the public during the Clerk's business hours, in the Two River Times legal ad section or online after the ordinance is introduced at a meeting of the Township Committee. Agendas are prepared by the Township Clerk and are posted in the Lobby of the Municipal Build-ing and on the website along with any ordinances scheduled for public hearings and Resolutions.

The Township Committee will take action on only those items listed on the agenda that is available to the public. Copies are available on the official bulletin board and at the lobby/entrance of the Main Meeting Room.

Typically, when you arrive at the meeting location, the clerk will have a process for public speakers to request time. There is probably a speaker slip that you fill out, indicating your name and which issue you are addressing (or if you're speaking to a non-agenda item). The clerk and the city website will have more details about the procedure and how much time each speaker is allowed.

Before you take the microphone, plan what you will say. Practice it. Time it. Make sure you can say the most important things within the allotted time. The most effective speakers are often the most succinct. State your name, your connection to the issue, and your "ask." Then if needed and if time permits, you can add a bit more. But especially if there are many speakers, don't try to fill your whole time if you don't have to.

> Good evening. My name is Jan Hsu and I have three children who play soccer in OurTown. I support the proposal to put eco-turf on the soccer field. My kids would be safer, and my life would be less stressful if we had artificial turf at Pele Park. We could plan with more certainty when the field will be available for practices and games, and we would know our kids wouldn't risk injury sliding in dirt and rocks like happens now as the grass wears out. I trust the staff to find the best product for the best price. Please at least study the issue and make an investment in our community and our kids.

If you signed up to speak and there have already been six or eight speakers before you, basically saying the same thing you planned to say, please don't give your whole prepared pitch anyway. Try something like this instead:

> My name is Sal Broome. I'm one of the many parents here who support safe, environmentally responsible landscape management in our public spaces. You've already heard from many speakers in support of this proposal. I'm with them. Thank you.

The protocol for public meetings is that speakers address the decision-makers, not the audience. This is not the time or place for a rally. Some groups organize rallies outside their city hall before a meeting, hoping to attract media attention. But inside the council chamber, there is a business meeting taking place. Your intent should be to inform the decision-makers to influence their decisions. Stunts and disruptions can backfire and annoy the people whose support you are hoping to win.

At each stage in the process, if you see progress, make note of it and acknowledge those that made it possible. Elected officials receive far more negative communications than positive ones. A simple "thank you, I'm glad you listened and took action" can go a long way. You could even consider coming to the next meeting after the council voted your way and use the non-agenda portion of the meeting to give a quick thank you in public.

Social Media

To Get on the Agenda

Look at your local newspapers and other media outlets and find out who their editors are. See what their guidelines are for opinion pieces and for letters to the editor. Typically, a commentary might be 500-1000 words while a letter to the editor is usually limited to 150-200 words.

Here is a sample letter to the editor if you are unable to get your issue on the city council's agenda. This is only eighty-six words long.

> For months, I have been trying to get the attention of our city council on the matter of [pesticides in our parks; safer turf on our soccer fields; reducing accidents on our streets] by asking them to put this issue on a council agenda. No luck. What are they afraid of? Who is blocking it? The residents deserve

a chance to present our request for action and to hear from our elected leaders. If you agree, call or email the council at [insert email and phone].

Once You Are on the Agenda

Find out the deadline for submitting written comments ahead of time and ask fellow supporters to express their support to the full deliberative body, on the record. It can be as simple as an email (most have a generic email like "citycouncil@city.state.gov") like Jacinta's other mom friends wrote.

> I'm writing in support of agenda item X, banning toxic pesticides in public parks. We are so lucky and appreciative of all the public spaces the city has provided and protected, but I share a concern over my children's health. Please insist that your contractors follow established procedures and work on a complete ban. If necessary, a good first step would be to do a pilot project in Central Town Park. Thanks.

Copy the city clerk on such messages and ask that your communication be included in the public record, so the report to the council will include correspondence received ahead of time and show the wide range of supporters. And be mindful that your message will be a public record, so write it with the readers' possible reaction in mind. Civility, clarity, communication.

After Your Hearing

If you feel satisfied with the outcome of your efforts, be sure to thank those who voted for your solution and the staff who helped get them there. This should be both private (e.g., a handwritten note or a personal email) and public. It is good for people to know that change can happen locally without massive protests or revolutionary upheavals. A commentary in a local publication as well as posts on social media can convey both appreciation for the specific results and optimism and encouragement to others to get more involved.

If you are not satisfied, be careful about using social media. You may still have a chance to get what you want, and you don't want to poison your relationships. Take what you can learn from those who opposed your efforts and go back to your analysis of the problem, the stakeholders (were there unexpected entities speaking in opposition), and your case statement, and see if there is room to revise and try again.

A wise friend said we need to "be the river" and learn how to flow around the rocks. This applies to social media usage. If you submit a letter to the editor or a longer commentary and the paper does not choose to print it, you can still post it on your social media outlets as an "open letter" to whoever you've identified as the obstacles.

Social media can be a powerful tool to address the obstacles that may have kept you from your goal. Maybe there was misinformation presented--a letter to the editor or opinion piece could clarify, correct, and reiterate the strong basis for your position. If the opposition comes from ignorance or different priorities, maybe you need to use social media to make the case for why your project is more important than recognized. Do you have data about how many people would benefit, or ideas about how to reduce the costs or otherwise address whatever obstacles were in the way?

We have said several times that government works slowly, but it does work. It's discouraging when you don't get what you wanted on the first try. But if you have a strong case and you have the time and energy to keep going, don't give up. Try to really listen and analyze what kept the decision-makers from doing what you asked. Revisit your problem statement and your case statement and see if there is a different way to frame the issue or a different approach to solving it. Most things aren't easy, but the effort is worthwhile.

In Conclusion

Don't be afraid to try

Treat everyone with civility and respect

Be patient

If you succeed, keep going, stay engaged

If you don't succeed, keep going, stay engaged

If you decide to run for office yourself … see our next book

ABOUT THE AUTHORS

Lisa Shaffer

People often ask why I ran for city council and just as many ask why I didn't run for a second term try for mayor or some other office. I had no long-term plan to run for any elected office. In fact, I'm much better suited to be in the administration than to be a politician. I'm blunt and sometimes short-tempered. I have strong opinions that I can express forcefully, and I am terrible at pretending to like someone who I don't respect. While I work at it, I don't always listen to understand as opposed to listening until it's my turn so I can try to persuade. Not good qualities in a politician.

How I got to city hall is probably not very important other than in the broadest terms. I met Teresa when she was running for city council some six years before I was elected. I was fairly new in town and thought it might be interesting to get involved. She was elected and I went to a city council meeting when she was sworn in. I was appalled at what I saw. The council members were disrespectful to each other and Roberts Rules of Order were abused and ignored and referred to as "non-binding guidance" rather than the agreed protocol.

After several years as an observer, I was getting more and more active and eventually another incumbent member, who was not going to be able to continue for health reasons, asked me to run. I thought about it, and I realized that someone would be occupying each of the five council seats, whether I ran or not. I could either keep complaining or I could reflect what I knew from Gandhi and "be the change" I wanted to see in my town. I also knew that I had already had several careers, had made whatever mark I was going to make, and was financially secure. So, I could run for office and whether or not I was elected, my life would go on and all would be well.

I had lived in my town for only seven years when I ran. I did not have deep roots or deep knowledge of local issues. But I knew there was discontent with the incumbents, and I ran on a platform with three promises: to work hard; play by the rules; and tell the truth. I had a lot of support from activists in the community who were also unhappy with the current regime and were not willing to run themselves. I did work hard, and I did follow all the arcane campaign finance rules as best I could without a professional campaign treasurer; and I told the truth. The truth was that I didn't have answers for a lot of issues, and I didn't know a lot (anything) about land use, zoning, affordable housing, the California Environmental Quality Act (CEQA) or much else at the local level. But my PhD in public policy and my forty years of work experience--including management, negotiations, marketing, and policy analysis--gave me the tools I could apply as I learned about city government.

I won. I came in first. I earned more votes than any candidate in the history of our town. The incumbent mayor came in fourth with only three seats available. I took office in December 2012.

Teresa Arballo Barth

I often said, "Community service is a family tradition." My father served on the local city council when I was young. My mother was active in a number of civic organizations and my sister and I were always expected to help.

I was engaged in the community and supported candidates for public office. However, serving on an elected board was never on my to-do list. Especially, since I had seen how the city council majority treated their colleague who often disagreed with them. She was trying to introduce more environmentally aware policies, community-sensitive development, and to encourage public involvement in the decision-making process. She was often the lone voice on the council, but she was speaking for many of us in the community.

Then one of the "gang of four," as we glibly called them, decided not to run for reelection. It is generally much easier to run for a vacant seat than it is to defeat an incumbent, and we saw an opportunity to win another seat on the city council.

After numerous strategy meetings, it became clear to me that everyone talked about the need for one of us to run for council, but no one was willing to do it. Many had a legitimate excuse: they had a full-time job, they had young children at home, etc. etc. etc. I had recently retired and had the time. I had worked for a large state agency and served on two county commissions; I was well versed in the bureaucracy side of government. I had name recognition and deep local roots. Friends and family were supportive, and the rest is history. I defeated the council's handpicked candidate and joined my friend on the council. We were still a minority voice, but we had a number of successes.

One of my goals was to change the "Good Old Boy" culture on the council and among city staff. I objected to the lackadaisical approach to how public notices were posted and council actions were reported (or not reported). I made an effort to show greater respect to my colleagues than they showed me, and the public began to see the difference. I am most proud of my efforts to create a more open and respectful city government.

Slowly, things began to improve. Unfortunately, my colleague was unable to complete her term due to ill health. The council majority appointed one of their own and I had become the lone voice. Except things were different this time. Many people openly criticized the behavior and actions of the council majority. One member was actually convicted for failing to disclose substantial gifts he had received (new kitchen appliances!) from an individual who had a code violation appeal before the council.

When the next election came around, Lisa Shaffer was elected. Happily, our reforms have continued, and the bar has been raised for local public office holders.

Acknowledgements

We want to thank many people who offered assistance and encouragement in this project. For reading various drafts and providing substantive and editorial input as well as moral support, Lois Sunrich, Marlena Medford, Rosemary Perlmeter, Judith Schnack, Elizabeth O'Conner, Dave Roberts, Tiffany Fox, Karen Brust, Nancy Westendorf, Kenneth Kales, and Alana Schuller. For providing input on how and when to use attorneys, Everett Delano, Marco Gonzalez, and Felix Tinkov. We thank Sharon Belknap for the illustrations, and Laura Beulke for layout and printing support.

Most important, for their love, patience, and support throughout our public service and beyond, we thank our husbands, Stephen Bartram and Don Barth, and our families. We were both inspired by the values and commitments of our parents, and we hope future generations will continue to engage in keeping our representative democracy more resilient, more just, and more compassionate.

References

American Planning Association: https://www.planning.org
American Public Works Association: https://www.apwa.net
Government Finance Officers Association: https://www.gfoa.org
http://mrsc.org/Home/Explore-Topics/Governance/Offices-and-Officers/Roles-and-Responsibilities.aspx
International City Managers Association: https://icma.org
International Institute of Municipal Clerks: https://www.iimc.com/268/About-Us
International Municipal Lawyers Association: https://imla.org
International Public Safety Association: https://www.joinipsa.org
League of Women Voters: https://www.lwv.org

Main Street America: https://www.mainstreet.org/home
National Association of City Transportation Officials: https://nacto.org
National Association of Counties: https://www.naco.org
National Information Officers Association: https://www.nioa.org
National League of Cities: https://www.nlc.org
National Recreation and Park Association: https://www.nrpa.org
United States Conference of Mayors: https://www.usmayors.org
What Are the Primary Functions of US Local Government? | Diligent Insights

Terminology

affordable housing—Definitions vary by jurisdiction. Typically housing available at a specified percentage of the local or regional median income.

agenda (some agencies call it a docket)—The formal order of items to be heard at a public meeting. States have open government rules defining when and how agendas are published. Agendas also explain the guidelines for public speakers.

appeal—A request to a higher authority to overturn the decision of a lower body (e.g., from a planning commission to a city council).

circulation—Refers to how people and goods move within and through the jurisdiction. Covers vehicles, pedestrians, and cyclists.

city manager—The administrative leader of a city, typically selected by the elected city council members.

element—A section of the general plan. Typical elements include land use, circulation (traffic), housing, recreation, open space, public safety.

entitlement—"Legal rights conveyed by approvals from governmental entities to develop a property for a certain use, intensity, building type, or building placement." [from Urban Land Institute]

general plan—Overarching land use and planning document, sometimes called a "comprehensive" or "master plan." The general plan addresses the physical development of the land. All other land use regulations and decisions within the jurisdiction must conform to the general plan.

hearing—A public meeting intended to obtain public testimony or comment before significant decisions are made. A public hearing can occur as part of a regular or special public meeting or, in some circumstances, can be entirely separate from a public meeting.

mayor—The most senior elected official. Mayors have varying degrees of authority and autonomy depending on the form of city government (i.e., strong mayor or strong city manager). Some cities rotate the mayoral responsibility among elected council members, others elect the mayor directly.

permit—A formal approval from a municipal government to proceed with a project. Permits are granted after the city determines that the proposed project complies with applicable rules and regulations.

planning commission—Appointed or elected body that reviews and approves land use projects, such as housing and commercial developments. In smaller jurisdictions, the city council may also serve as the planning commission.

public record—Public records are information or documents created by a government agency or officer and are required by law to be stored and maintained. This can include correspondence with members of the public.

public works—"Public works is the combination of physical assets, management practices, policies, and personnel necessary for government to provide and sustain structures and services essential to the welfare and acceptable quality of life for its citizens." [from American Public Works Association]

warrants—For city government, the term "warrant" can mean a commitment to expend funds. It can mean the justification for an action, whether an arrest warrant or warrants to justify placement of a stop sign.

zoning—How governments control the physical development of land and define the types of uses allowed. Typical zoning categories include residential, commercial, recreational, light or heavy industry, open space, and mixed use.

[1] It's Complicated: State and Local Government Relationships
[2] The State-Local Fiscal Relationship
[3] 23 Code of Federal Regulations 655 - FHWA MUTCD
[4] https://www.nlc.org/resource/cities-101-delegation-of-power
[5] State and Local Governments [ushistory.org]
[6] Mayoral Powers
[7] Federal, Regional and Local Jurisdiction Projects & Planning
[8] Overview
[9] Sales Tax Rates in Major Cities, 2019 | Local Sales Taxes
[10] Tax Policy Center
[11] https://www.ca-ilg.org/sites/main/files/file-attachments/resources__finalbook_0.pdf
[12] Comprehensive Plans
[13] Land Use 101
[14] Transportation Planning
[15] Pesticides | US EPA
[16] Affordable Apartments in California | CHW
[17] Home - California Building Industry Association | CBIA
[18] Municipal Codes: A Beginner's Guide | In Custodia Legis: Law Librarians of Congress]
[19] https://www.californiacityclerks.org
[20] The Balanced Triangle and the City Clerk's Role in Local Government
[21] State Law Resources
[22] State Law Resources